T0103905

A Mountain of MANY NAMES

LLOYD HOLM

www.trafford.com
North America & international
toll-free: 1 888 232 4444 (USA & Canada)
fax: 812 355 4082

Contents

Preface...vii

Blue Canyon 1
Adventures at Big Bend 10
    Introduction 10
    The Rescue...10
    If You Ain't Makin' Mistakes,
    You Ain't Doing Nothing! 14
    Some Afterthoughts.. 26

Bessie and Me Ramblings of a Lookout 28
    Foreward 28
    Butte Falls... 28
    My Introduction to Bessie 30
    The Rock and My House 36
    A Day in the Life of a Lookout 40
    The Break 49
    Fire in the Mountains! 50
    Goodbye Bessie 56
    Afterwards..59
    Afterthoughts..62

"Thirty-Four Degrees Year 'Round" 64
    Introduction 64
    The Crew... 64
    The Task 65

The Water 67
Many Years Later 68

Misfire 69
The Perfect Day 78
A Mountain Of Many Names 84

Preface

"A Mountain of Many Names" refers to Mt. McLoughlin, a 9,965-foot dormant volcano located in southern Oregon. My introduction to the mountain was in 1957 on my first trip to a little town nestled in the Cascade Range of Oregon called Butte Falls. As we drove through Agate Desert (now White City) Claude Curtis pointed out the mountain and I instantly fell in love with it. I have lived and worked in its shadow most of my life. During my time with the United States Forest Service I became the Cultural Resource Technician for the Butte Falls Ranger District. I was able to research the many names the mountain has had, both Native American and English. I came up with 15 names, give or take. Thus the name of my book.

I did not start out to write a book. I wanted to tell the story of my first year here in Butte Falls as a record for my family. That was to be the end of it. As I researched historical records and old photos I found myself recalling more and more of my early life. Memories came flooding back and the story got longer. Soon I was recalling events from my first 2 years with the Forest Service on the Big Bend District of the Tahoe National Forest. More stories were written and eventually I found I had enough to publish a small book.

I have mostly concentrated on stories that occurred early in my career because those were the most exciting. Those were the unusual jobs. The jobs that were never predictable and boring. What I call "Dream Jobs." Trail crew on horseback; a summer on a lookout; trail construction in a back-country wilderness. This book is the result of my musings.

As I wrote I began thinking of how things have changed since 1955 when I began my journey with the Forest Service. To most people today a trail means a recreation trail. A trail that goes to a lake or some other feature. A trail is a hiking or riding trail like the Pacific Crest Trail. Not so in 1955. Trails then were a vital part of the National Forest transportation system. They were the life-line for isolated lookouts and fire guard stations. They served for maintaining phone lines, and they provided access for fighting backcountry fires. Trails were used by pack strings of perhaps five or more mules and a horse. Yearly maintenance was critical. As roads were built deeper and deeper in to the forest, trails began to disappear and the purpose of those that remain has changed. Yes, a lot has changed.

I hope that those who read this enjoy it and that my children and grandchildren will get some idea of my life as a young man before they were born.

I wish to thank my wife Diane for her patience as I ignored her while I was typing away deep in thought, and for reading, editing and making suggestions on endless revisions. I also want to thank my favorite bartender Missy who read many of the stories, helped with the edits, and encouraged me. My heartfelt thanks go to Janice Shultz who took time from her busy schedule to edit my final revisions. She found many errors and made valuable suggestions. Thank you Janice. And of course my six sons and daughters, and my step-children who have to read this stuff simply because they are "family" and are the original target of this effort.

Finally, to my mother Eleanor (Holm) LeNeve goes my love and thanks. RIP Mom. No matter what endeavor I chose in life you supported and encouraged me. I am sure that no matter what success I have with this book you are proud of me. You always were.

Blue Canyon

In 1955 as my junior year at Nevada Union High School in Grass Valley, California was coming to an end, my mom urged me to find a summer job so I could help her with the household expenses. I was thinking more about lazy summer days swimming and hanging around with the boys, but mom was a go-getter and would have no part of that nonsense. She began calling around looking for work for me. Someone suggested she call the Forest Service so she called the Tahoe National Forest. They told her that if I was 18 years old, I should fill out an application and submit it to the Big Bend Ranger District where they maintained a fire crew at Blue Canyon and hired summer help. She requested an application and when it came she helped me fill it out. When we came to my age and birth date we lied. I was only 17 years old in 1955. We sent the form to Big Bend and waited. A week or so later I got a reply and a job offer. School was out on June 4, the job started in mid-June. Screwed up my lazy summer!

Mom drove me to Big Bend Ranger Station on the morning of June 13. I was really worried. At 17 years old with my blond hair and skinny body I looked about 15 years old. I was sure they would question my age and throw me in jail for lying on a federal form. They didn't. After filling out a couple perfunctory forms I said goodbye to mom and was transported about 10 miles down Highway 40 to the Blue Canyon Guard Station.

The Guard Station consisted of a small one-room cabin, an army tent set up on a wood platform, an enclosed outdoor shower and an outhouse. The cabin served as the kitchen and lounge area.

The tent had army cots set up and was the bedroom for the five crew members. Before the day was out all five showed up and we got acquainted. For transportation we had a "crummy" (a crew van) and the foreman's pickup. The pickup carried our tools, lunches etc.

Our foreman, Charles didn't stay with us. He was married, in his thirties and lived down the Highway at Colfax. He commuted and met us most days at the Guard Station. The rest of the crew was young; Dave was the oldest at 21. He was given the responsibility of supervising us when our foreman wasn't around. He was the only one that had a Forest Service driver's license so he was our crummy driver. Bob, who would become my best friend, was 18 years old; the others were 18 or 19. I'm sorry to say that I have forgotten their names.

Our first week was spent in training. We learned about forest fires, and how they are controlled. We learned about the tools we would use and how to use them safely and we spent days using the tools building practice fire lines around the Guard Station. Most of it was hard, dusty, boring work. Not at all what I had imagined the excitement of being a firefighter was all about.

During this time, Bob and I began to bond as friends. Bob had just graduated from Napa High School in Napa California. We both had the same interests and clicked right off the bat. Bob had a "54" Ford that he was customizing and it getting painted in Napa with custom, metal flaked, green paint. He couldn't wait until it was done so he could drive to the Guard Station and show me.

The crew's days off were staggered so someone would always be on duty. Bob and I arranged to have the same days off, Thursday and Friday. On our first days off we had no car, so on Thursday afternoon after getting bored hanging around the cabin, we decided to hitchhike about 30 miles down Highway 40 to Colfax and watch a movie. In those days hitchhiking was common. That has all changed.

Late that afternoon we easily caught a ride to Colfax. We ate dinner at the local hamburger joint and went to the theater. It was a double feature and we got out of the movie late, around midnight.

Traffic was slow on the highway and we had trouble flagging a ride back. After about an hour and a half a semi-rig pulled over and offered us a ride. Bob crawled behind the seats while I took the passenger seat. We told the driver we were going to Blue Canyon and he said he knew the spot. Before long I nodded off.

I awoke feeling someone fondling my crotch. It was the driver. I yelled, "Stop, let me out of here. Bob this guy's queer! Let's go!" (The word gay wasn't in use then.) Bob began yelling at the driver to stop. The guy found a barely passable place to pull off the highway and stop and Bob and I both scurried out of the rig. The truck was loaded and heavy and he had stopped on a hill. He had a hard time getting moving and up to speed again. As he struggled to get going Bob and I ran alongside and threw rocks at the fender and door.

I understand now, in this world where tolerance is the new watch word, that our behavior would be considered negative. In fact we could be accused of a hate crime in today's world. As I have aged I have mellowed and accept alternative life styles. But to understand our actions you have to understand the world as it was in 1955. As children we were taught that "queers" were perverts. They were evil and of no use to society. We were taught to avoid anyone that showed those tendencies and to turn them in to the cops. We were taught that by our parents and elders and we believed it. The world has changed!

Bob and I now had to flag down another ride and since we were both sleeping when the incident happened we weren't sure where we were. Had we passed Blue Canyon? We didn't know. We shortly got a ride by a man and woman and got to Blue Canyon a few miles up the road. We were late to bed, but we had the next day off.

The next week Bob went home to Napa and picked up his newly painted Ford. He was proud as punch when he returned, and we all went out to admire the glistening metal flaked paint job. Bob couldn't tolerate any dust on his new paint, but since the road into Guard Station was six inches deep with dust it become a daily ritual for Bob to wash his car after hours. I was there to give him a hand. Now we wouldn't have to hitchhike, we had wheels!

Sometime in early July we got a call. It would be a life changing day. There had been an accident near Soda Springs Ski Lodge. We were given orders to proceed a short distance up in the hills from the Lodge to some meadow at the headwaters of the South Fork Yuba River and aid in any way possible. Details about what had happened were sketchy, but it had to do with someone falling in the river.

Our foreman was off that day so Dave was in charge. Our training had paid off and the entire crew was in the Crummy and on the way in just a few minutes. It was less than a quarter-mile to Highway 40, and from there it was about 10 or 12 miles up the highway to Soda Springs near Donner Summit. In those days few Forest Service vehicles had sirens or emergency lights and we had none, so Dave proceeded as fast and safely as he could, weaving in and out of traffic on the then two-lane highway. As we traveled, Dave explained that he was an Eagle Scout and had some training for emergency situations. He asked if any of the rest of the crew had any of those skills. As it turned out I was the only one. I had made it to First Class as a Scout and was working on my merit badges to get to Eagle Scout. One of the merit badges I had earned was on water safety and I had learned to do artificial respiration.

We were at the Soda Springs junction in about 15 minutes where we met a car that led us to the scene of the accident. About a mile from the ski lodge up a dirt road we came to a meadow where a station wagon and Forest Service pickup were parked.

As we hurriedly exited the Crummy we could see Assistant District Ranger Roger Brown giving artificial respiration to a small child about 3 years old who was lying on a blanket. An obviously distraught man and woman stood nearby. The man explained that they had arrived at the meadow, and while he and his wife were unloading the station wagon and preparing for a summer picnic the child had wandered away. They noticed he was gone and began searching for him and found him floating in the river. They pulled him out and one of the pair quickly drove to Soda Springs Lodge for help. The people at the lodge called the Forest Service and the nearest doctor and ambulance, but that was in Reno about an hour away. By the time we got there at least a half-hour had elapsed.

Roger said he needed a break, and he needed to get to his pickup to call the Ranger Station on his radio to update them and find out the status of the doctor. He asked for a volunteer to continue the artificial respiration. Dave responded.

As Dave worked the rest of us kneeled by the child and rubbed his body to hopefully provide warmth and help his circulation. One of the crew put his ear near the child's mouth and said he could hear air movement and others would say they felt warmth in his body. Remarks like that gave the parents some hope. But hope was all they had. What they really wanted was a smiling, happy child.

After about 10 minutes Dave asked me to take over his job. You need to understand that things have changed a lot since 1955. It had not yet been discovered that mouth-to-mouth resuscitation was the most effective artificial respiration. What we were doing was straddling the child while placing our hands on his back and pushing down to provide a pumping effect. As we pumped we kept a rhythm by reciting "Out goes the bad air," as we pressed down, and "In goes the good air," as we relaxed. This method was effective if you got to the victim relatively soon after he had got water into his lungs, but mouth-to-mouth is much more effective if time has elapsed. Unfortunately we didn't know that then.

I took over for Dave and began pumping. Meanwhile Roger had contacted the Ranger Station and updated them. The estimated ETA for the doctor was 10 to 20 minutes. Ten minutes later Dave relieved me. As I rested I looked at the parents and could read the dread on their faces. It was a very somber atmosphere as we waited for the doctor.

We could hear a vehicle approaching and soon an ambulance came into view. Understand that ambulances then were strictly for transporting patients. They weren't loaded with emergency lifesaving gear as they are now. There was no oxygen.

The doctor quickly exited with his stethoscope. Kneeling by the child he first lifted his eyelids and checked his eyes. Then he searched for a heartbeat from the back. He turned the child over and carefully checked for a beat on his chest. Slowly he rose to his knees and looked at the parents, "I'm sorry. There's nothing we can do now."

All they heard was "I'm sorry." A mournful scream came from the woman as she began to collapse. Roger caught her and held her close to his chest. The man lowered his head and loudly sobbed with his hands to his face. These are things I will never forget.

The doctor went to the woman and laid her down on a blanket as he tried his best to help her. Roger got on the radio to arrange a ride for the parents to Reno where the child would be taken. Then he arranged for someone to drive their station wagon as it was obvious they could not drive. Bob and I walked to the river where the child was found. It hardly deserved the name river; it was more like a brook. The child was found in a slow moving spot about 2 feet deep and 3 feet wide. The high mountain water was very cold, probably 40 degrees or lower and that no doubt had stunned the child and delayed any reaction he might have made to get out.

When all of the arrangements were made there was no more use for us. Roger released us. It was a quiet, somber drive back to Blue Canyon. Someone said, "The child was dead when we got there." It was probably true, but it didn't help us. We had prayed that we could save that child and no matter how you put it, it seemed that we had failed. The mournful scream from that woman echoed in my mind.

Back at Blue Canyon it was a quiet afternoon. Most of us split up to be alone with our thoughts. I found a large pine tree away from the cook-shack and sat on the ground with my back to it. As I gazed around all I could see was vibrant life; trees and birds, pine squirrels scurrying around the ground and up the trunks of the trees, bees humming.

This was my first close experience with death and it was humbling. As I sat there I vowed that if I ever had children I would never let them around water unattended. It had taken only a few short minutes for that beautiful child to fall in shallow water and die. I wanted to never to see that again.

We were off duty at 6 p.m. and Bob found me and said, "C'mon Lloyd let's get the hell out of here."

We piled in his Ford and drove away. "Want to go to Grass Valley and get something to eat." Bob said.

"Sounds great, anywhere is fine." I answered.

Grass Valley is about 40 miles away down Highway 20, which intersects Highway 40 very near Blue Canyon. Highway 20 in those days was a pretty lonely road. It was even lonelier that day. We hardly spoke as he drove. Neither one of us wanted to talk about the day's events.

In about an hour we reached Nevada City. There was traffic and all the normal activity you're used to, and that helped to pull our minds back to the present. In another 4 miles we were in Grass Valley. We went to a popular teen hangout where we hoped to see girls. It was a fast-food restaurant where you could walk in and get a table and play the juke box, or drive in and get served in your car. We chose to go inside.

We each ordered a hamburger, fries and a shake then played some of our favorite songs on the juke box. Settled in, we began scanning the place for girls. Bob was a pretty good looking guy with an Elvis haircut, and it wasn't long before two girls in an adjoining table began to talk with him. A short time later we moved to their table.

We made all the normal chat. What grade are you in? Where do you live? You have a job? Who is you favorite singer? And so on. One of the girls asked that if we were firefighters what did we do when not fighting fires? It immediately took me back to the day's events. What do we do when not fighting fires? We fail! I could see that Bob was affected too.

The girls would both be juniors next year. They were cute and they liked us. They ask if we wanted to go to one of the girls place and spin some records. Normally that would be the invitation we would jump at, but I looked at Bob and he looked at me and we silently agreed. "Damn, we got to go to work early tomorrow and got a long drive. Maybe we could make it another time." Bob said.

We hung around with them another half hour, took names and phone numbers, then said our goodbyes and headed back to Blue Canyon. As we rode back in the dark neither of us spoke until we were about 5 miles from the Guard Station when Bob said aloud to no one, "I never want to do that again!" I remained silent. It didn't require an answer.

It took at least a week for things to return to normal at the Guard Station and during that time our foreman ask me if I wanted to help him take supplies to the lookout at Grouse Ridge. I jumped at the chance to get away from the boredom of the Guard Station and see some new country. The next day Charley picked me up early in the morning with a pickup already loaded with food, batteries, propane, and white gas and office supplies for the lookout. As I recall Grouse Ridge was about 20 miles from the Guard Station and the last 10 miles was rough, rocky dirt road. After about an hour of bouncing around the pickup, and backing up to take another run at a steep grade we finally made it to the lookout.

Grouse Ridge lookout is at 7700 feet elevation and the view is awesome. It was manned by a sweet older couple that was happy to have visitors. We unloaded our cargo and the woman insisted she cook us lunch. As we sat there eating I was full of questions for the pair. It was my first time on a lookout and I was impressed and thought that someday I would like to do it. Little did I know that in 2 years that dream would come true?

In August, we responded to our first fire of the season. A lightning strike had hit a power pole and sparks from the broken line had started a fire near Spaulding Lake road not far from our Guard Station. By the time we got there a tanker truck had arrived and had the 3-acre blaze pretty much under control. We were set to work putting a fire-line around the fire. As I worked I got into a yellow jackets nest and was stung three times. One sting was near my right eye, another on my right arm and one on my back. By the time we got back to our station my eye was swollen shut and my arm looked like a balloon. Our foreman told me to take a few days off until the swelling went down. I didn't want to hang around the Guard Station so I hitch-hiked to my home in Grass Valley. It was kind of weird hitching. When someone stopped to give me a ride they saw the grotesque swelling on my face and arm and I had to quickly explain what had happened. Fortunately no one refused me a ride.

The last major event of that summer was in late August. A fire started on the Nevada City Ranger District in very steep terrain and grew to over 2000 acres. Our crew was sent there to help. When we got there we were assigned to a night crew on the bottom of the fire. Our job was to patrol the hand fire-line. It was very steep terrain and we were to watch for and control any live fire that rolled down the hill and over the fire-line. There was another crew in the same area and occasionally we took our breaks with them. I found out that they were a convict crew. They were from a prison work center and apparently or hopefully were trustworthy. I got to know several of them and they seemed like your everyday normal laborer. I didn't have any fear working with them.

By September my time was getting short. I had to return to high school in the first week of the month. I said goodbye to my friends and Bob gave me a ride home in his shiny metal-flaked green Ford. Bob and I traded addresses and we would keep in touch over the next few years. It had been a very intense summer.

Adventures at Big Bend

INTRODUCTION

"If you don't make mistakes you aren't doing anything." That old adage is pregnant with truth. We all make mistakes, and in many ways they are good for us. It's from our mistakes that we learn. I made mistakes as a young man and I learned from them. In the two stories that follow you will see what I mean.

THE RESCUE

In 1956 I graduated from High School in Grass Valley, California. Upon graduating I started my second summer with the Forest Service on the Blue Canyon Fire Crew; but about a week into the season the District needed a trail crew member and selected me. I was moved up the highway near Donner Summit to the Ranger Station at Big Bend. My new quarters was a small cabin behind the Ranger Station that I shared with Terry, my companion on the trail crew. Terry was 19 years old, a year older than me.

Terry and I spent our first week or so doing campground cleanup and maintenance around the Ranger Station and along the South Fork of the Yuba River as we waited for our boss and horse wrangler to show up. It was good work and less restricting than being on the fire crew. I had high hopes for a fun summer.

One evening after supper one of the foresters came to our cabin and enlisted us to join a rescue crew. There was an injured man at Lola Montez Lakes that needed assistance.

A frightened and wet woman had showed up at the Ranger Station around 7:30 p.m. and said that she and her companion had hiked into the Lola Montez lakes area and he had hurt his ankle. Somehow he had hobbled and crawled to a lake hoping someone would be camped there, but no help was there and he could go no further. The woman had never been in a wilderness situation before. He explained to her that she would have to go for help. He told her to follow the trail from the lake and it would come out at Big Bend Campground where she could get help at the nearby Ranger Station.

At that elevation there were still large snow drifts around. He told her that if she lost the trail in the snow to continue downhill where she would come to the upper reaches of the South Yuba River. If she waded across the river she would come to Highway 40; the main route between Reno and Sacramento. There she could flag a car down and get a ride to Big Bend. (Highway 40 then was a two lane road. It is now I-80.)

The poor woman did lose the trail and continued downhill over rough, rocky and brushy terrain. She eventually found the river and the highway. By the time she got to Big Bend she was wet; her clothes were in tatters and she was badly scratched from the brush. She feared that wild animals were stalking her and worried about ever making it to safety. She was in tears most of the way. The folks at the Ranger Station calmed her down, treated her wounds and gave her a warm heavy shirt to wear. They assured her that a rescue team would be sent for her husband. They then transported her up the highway a few miles to Soda Springs Ski Lodge where a warm meal and a room were waiting for her.

That's when we were recruited. There were six men on the crew led by Assistant District Ranger Roger Brown who was familiar with the Lola Montez Lakes area. One man carried a pack with C-rations and emergency first-aid gear. The rest of us took turns carrying a stretcher.

It was near dusk when we left and began the 3-mile mostly uphill hike to the first Lola Montez Lake. There were two, the Upper and the Lower. Before long we were hiking in the dark over snowdrifts and wading across ice cold, swollen streams with unstable footing. At night with flashlights it was difficult keeping on the trail especially where there were long stretches of snow. Roger went ahead and scouted it out. We followed, marking it with red plastic ribbon to find on our way out.

Roughly 90 minutes later we came to Lower Lola Montez Lake. In the dark we saw no activity, so someone loudly yelled, "Hello."

"I'm here!" Came an answer.

We began making our way around the lakeshore and when we got clear of some large boulders and trees we could see the glow of a fire across the lake. In about 10 minutes we approached a man lying on the ground near the fire. We were all a bit surprised to see that he was Chinese.

Roger asked, "Are you John?"

"Yes." he answered, "My God! She made it!

"Yes and besides being a little scared, she's OK. What's wrong with your leg?

"I think my ankle is broken. I was so worried about Sarah, I wasn't sure she had the know how to make it"

"She's OK. Look, everybody get some rest, get warm and dry out. I'll look at his leg. Then we have to decide if we want to carry him out tonight or wait until daybreak."

Roger inspected John's ankle and determined it was indeed broken. The first aid kit was equipped with an ankle splint and Roger was able to get it around his leg and stabilize the bone without too much pain. We made some instant coffee and ate a few candy bars. John told us they had driven up from San Francisco for a day hike into the lakes and weren't equipped for camping.

After consulting everyone Roger decided the best course of action was to get John out as soon as possible. He decided to carry him out that night. It was around 10 p.m.

John was a fairly large man, around 180 or 190 pounds. With our help he was able to scoot on the stretcher and a blanket was tucked around him. Four of us carried the stretcher, one man went ahead to scout out the easiest route and one man stayed by the stretcher to help if one or the other side took on more weight. That occasionally happened as we crossed boulders or streams. About every 10 minutes we rested and the scout and extra hand traded jobs with two men on the stretcher. Crossing one knee-deep stream was a real chore and everyone helped with the stretcher and we got him across safe and dry. John was a trooper and never complained. The trail was much easier to find since we had marked it with ribbons on the way up. After about 2 ½ hours we made it to the Ranger Station. We were exhausted but no one was hurt and John was no worse for the wear.

Roger called a hospital in Reno and an ambulance was dispatched. It would be at Big Bend in an hour. Then he called Soda Springs to give the woman the message that John had been rescued and that he was being sent to a hospital.

We all lounged around the Rangers office as we waited for the ambulance. John was still on the stretcher which had been placed on a mattress someone had found. Rogers's wife had brought coffee and donuts in and we were all feeling smug about our good deed that night. At least I was. I got a bright idea!

"Hey, why don't we call the San Francisco Chronicle and give them the story about how we rescued one of their citizens in the wilds of the High Sierras!" Wouldn't that be neat?"

Suddenly John reared up his head and shoulders, and yelled, "No! Please don't do that! That's not my wife!"

Oops!

Roger gave me one of those "Nice going!" looks and tried to calm John, "Don't worry John; no one is going to call the paper! Are we Lloyd?" He said while glaring at me.

But John had sensed that I was eager for fame. In his mind he saw himself and his mistress in blaring newspaper headlines. He kept pleading, "Please, please, don't tell the newspapers!"

So Roger spent the rest of the time until the ambulance came assuring poor John that no one was calling anyone. Finally, Roger released me and Terry. Told us to go to bed and since we had had a hard night we didn't need to work the next day.

Back at our cabin Terry couldn't stop laughing. "Ha, ha, ha you really blew it Lloyd, ha, ha, ha." All of my smugness evaporated. Terry would never let me live that one down. I learned something that night. If you don't know all of the facts, KEEP YOUR MOUTH SHUT!!

If You Ain't Makin' Mistakes, You Ain't Doing Nothing!

Our foreman showed up a week or so after the rescue. Rex was a short, stocky, bow-legged man in his mid-forties. He looked every bit the cowboy. A large cattle ranch in Nevada had contracted with the Forest Service to supply a wrangler and horses for the short trail-maintenance season every summer. This was Rex's third year at Big Bend. He brought with him four horses, which were kept at a small barn and corral near the Ranger Station along with Betsy, the Forest Service pack horse. Rex moved in to a cabin at Soda Springs, a short distance from Big Bend.

His first job was to familiarize Terry and me with the job, and the horses. Terry's uncle owned a ranch on the Rogue River near the Table Rocks in Oregon. At 15 years old Terry began visiting and working with his uncle every summer. He learned to ride and herd cattle and was a pretty capable horseman. I'm the greenhorn. Except for riding a horse on a merry-go-round I had never been on a saddle, much less a live horse.

Rex fixed me up with Jerry, a dark bay gelding. He was a gentle, well trained horse that Rex thought I could handle. I learned to bridal and saddle him and rode him around Big Bend campground to learn his habits. I felt comfortable and safe riding him and Rex was satisfied with my performance. Terry had Romper, a black gelding and a much more spirited horse than Jerry. Terry, with his experience, handled him with ease. Rex had brought two horses for himself; his favorite dark stallion Midnight, and Prince, a tall, lanky, dun-colored stallion known for eccentric behavior. Prince was an unknown quantity and Rex had brought him to see if he could be trained for the work we were doing. On our first training ride through the forest as a team, Prince, in spite of Rex's reining, ran headlong into a tree ingloriously dumping Rex to the ground. Rex cussed the horse and the earth he stood on and gave up on "that stupid son-of-a-bitch!" That was the last day Prince would have a saddle on. He was sentenced to the corral at Big Bend.

After two days of training we started our first real job. We were to maintain Lola Montez trail from Big Bend to a place called Peter Grubb Hut. It was a one-day job so we took no camping gear.

Rex led the way as we started up the trail from Big Bend Campground. Terry followed and I brought up the rear leading Betsy who carried our tools and lunches. Betsy was a short, wide-bodied, dappled gray mare. Not much to look at but she had positive attributes. She was very tractable, and had been over these trails before. She knew the country well. Before the summer was over I would be impressed at how good a horse's memory is. Betsy was so knowledgeable it was almost like having a second foreman. Terry and I fell in love with her and Rex had nothing but praise for her.

As we came upon rocks we dismounted and rolled them out. The horses were well trained for this kind of work, when you dropped their reins they just stood around eating what little grass they could find along the trail. The first time we stopped Rex gave me instructions on how to keep my two charges together.

"Drape Betsy's lead rope over Jerry's saddle horn and let it drape to the ground like this. Don't tie a knot!" He said while showing me. "Keep a watch on it and if Betsy pulls the rope off, go back and redo it."

I was surprised that he didn't wrap the rope around the saddle horn and tie it in a knot, which would have kept the horses together and eliminated the need to continually interrupt my work to tend to the horses and the rope, but I kept my thoughts to myself. About every 10 minutes or so Betsy or Jerry would wander away seeking another blade of grass and the rope would drop to the ground. I would have to go back, gather up the horses and start the game again.

We slowly worked our way up the trail rolling boulders out, fixing erosion ditches, lopping off limbs that had grown in the trailway, and cutting out fallen trees. I wondered what would happen with the horses when we first started the chainsaw. I expected them to bolt and run, but the first time we did they didn't blink an eye. Rex said they all had worked around machinery, especially chainsaws, before and were accustomed to sudden loud noises.

"It's a good group of animals we got here!"

We made it to Lower Lola Montez Lake (the same lake where Terry and I had helped with the rescue of John) where we took a break. We finally got to see it in the daytime. The lake is over 7000 feet elevation in sub-alpine terrain. With crystal clear water and mountain scenery it's absolutely beautiful. We poured coffee from our thermos, took a seat on the rocks with a snack and enjoyed the sun and scenery.

A short distance later we came to Upper Lola Montez Lake; smaller than the lower one but just as beautiful. There were a few snow drifts around the lake. Occasionally as we traveled along we caught views of Castle Peak; a large mountain with three separate spires rising over 9100 feet.

As we worked I marveled at how lucky I was. As a child I dreamed about riding in the high country like the Mountain Men that I had read about and admired. This was more like a vacation than work and I was enjoying every minute of it. With every mile I was learning more about horses and getting more comfortable in the saddle.

We worked our way up to Peter Grubb Hut. It was at the edge a beautiful meadow near the base of Castle Peak.

Peter Grubb was a young lad of 18 years old who died in 1937, the year I was born. He loved the high mountains and cross-country skiing. His family, along with the Sierra Club built the cabin for a wilderness shelter as a memorial to him. When we were there anyone could use it for free, though I believe it's been highly commercialized since.

Peter Grubb Hut was the end of our trail work. We secured all of our tools in Betsy's packs and began the trip back. It was a carefree trip. Rex told stories of his adventures, and we joked and laughed as we ambled our way down the trail to Big Bend. Terry and I were getting acquainted with Rex and felt at ease with him. It would be a good summer.

When we got back to Big Bend our first job, as always, was to tend to the animals. We unsaddled and inspected them carefully, looking for sore spots. We turned them out in the corral and fed them some hay. Each horse got a feedbag of oats as a reward for a job well done. Then we stored our tack in the barn. With that our day was done. On the trail crew it mattered not what time of day it was. When you got the job done you were off for the rest of the day.

We began planning for our next trip of 4 days working several trails. We made a list of food, cooking gear and tools we needed. Most of our cooking gear was rounded up at Big Bend. The few things we couldn't find we put on our shopping list, and the next day the three of us went over Donner Pass about 20 miles to the small town of Truckee to buy food and supplies. Back at Big Bend we loaded our supplies in Betsy's packs and our saddle bags. We were ready to go, and Terry and I went to bed anxious to begin our first extended trip.

Up at dawn the next morning we were at the corral saddling and packing the animals. It was a bright sunny morning as we mounted our horses and worked our way down to Highway 40. We would have to cross the highway to reach the trailhead on the other side. Normally it's a busy road; the main route between the San Francisco Bay Area and the popular gambling Mecca of Reno, but the early morning traffic is lighter and we managed to scurry the horses across safely. We worked our way down the side of the highway until we came to the trailhead.

We began working our way up a steep trail to the top of the southern high ridges of the South Fork Yuba River. The trail was so strewn with debris that Rex and Terry gave up riding their horses and walked while kicking out rocks and limbs. I rode while leading Betsy. At one point Betsy balked and no amount of urging on my part could make her move. Rex knew in an instant that there was a rattlesnake nearby.

"Betsy can smell a rattler and ain't movin' an inch 'til it's gone or dead."

Rex and Terry went ahead a short way and tied their horses to a tree then walked back towards me carefully searching for the snake. They finally scared it up below the trail. They killed it with a large boulder and tossed it a good way off the trail. Good ole' Betsy had another useful skill!

In the glaring sun it was hot, dusty work and we spent 4 or 5 hours clearing the relatively short distance to the top of the ridge. Once there we came upon a large meadow with a wide, clear stream running through it. The trail split here; one branch going east then south to the Royal Gorge of the American River, and the other heading west toward Devils Peak. Rex said, "We camp here tonight."

We found a shady place under some firs at the edge of the meadow and unloaded Betsy's packs. We unsaddled the horses, hobbled them and after a handful of oats turned them out in the meadow where they were content grazing on the lush grass.

A large fire ring was built. We placed our grill over it and brewed up a pot of camp coffee. The three of us took a seat on a log and ate a late lunch swishing it down with our coffee. We decided that with the fair weather we didn't need to put up a shelter. Sleeping under the trees would keep most of the dew off our bags. After our break we put a large tarp on the ground near the fire, inflated our air mattresses and rolled out our sleeping bags; then gathered enough firewood for the night.

It was still early, around 4 o'clock, and Terry and I were a couple of happy teens full of spunk and energy. We asked Rex if we could take the horses for a bare-back ride a mile or so down the Royal Gorge trail.

"I reckon so. You rode bare-back before?" He asked.

"Oh yeah." Terry said, "Lots of time at my uncle's place."

"OK. Lloyd you take Betsy for your first time. She rides gentle and is easy to handle."

So we rounded up our horses and bridled them and Terry gave me a few lessons on how to mount a horse bare-back. After a few tries I got the hang of it. We trotted the horses through the meadow down to the trail, and as soon as we were out of sight of camp Terry kicked Romper into a full gallop and down the trail he went. I followed suit pushing Betsy to a gallop and damn near fell off! I learned to get the motion of my body in sync with Betsy's rolling gallop and was soon riding bare-back like a pro.

Romper was the faster horse so I was losing ground when we came to the creek that flowed out of the meadow. It was about eight feet wide and a foot deep. Terry spurred his horse and Romper leapt the creek with room to spare. I followed suit. I leaned over with my head alongside of Betsy's neck, prepared for the jump that was sure to come. Except it didn't! Betsy came to a screeching halt at the edge of the stream, but I kept going. Flying over Betsy's head smack-dab into the middle of the creek! Betsy just stood there and watched.

Nothing was hurt except my pride, so a sopping wet Lloyd got up and began wading out of the creek as Betsy gave me a quizzical look. Just then Terry came riding back to see what had happened and after establishing that I wasn't hurt had a hearty laugh. There was nothing for me to do but laugh with him. I got Betsy back to some level ground and mounted her and she waded gingerly across the creek. We continued down the trail at a full gallop whopping and hollering like Indians. About a mile down the trail we turned and headed back at a walk as we rested the horses. We talked and laughed and enjoyed the mountain air. Back at the creek Terry again jumped his horse across, but I was wiser now and let Betsy have her head. Once more she gingerly picked her way across. We trotted the horses back to camp, let them out in the meadow to graze, and took our seat by the fire.

Rex asked, "How'd it go boys?"

That was the opening the Terry was waiting for. "Man, it was so funny! Betsy dumped Lloyd in the creek when he tried to jump her across!"

Rex laughed. "Yup, I shudda' told you 'bout that. Ole' Betsy don't like to jump. She prefers to pick her way across obstacles."

"Well," I said. "I was hot and dusty and wanted to take a bath anyway. Betsy was just helping me." We all had a good laugh.

We had a late dinner of fire grilled steaks, coal roasted potatoes and a big can of beans and of course, the ever-present coffee. Around the fire after dinner Rex laid out his plans for the next day. We would work our way the 6 or so miles down to the Royal Gorge of the American River and make camp by the stream.

"My favorite place. It's a beautiful spot. Good fishin' down there. Not too big, but they'll make a nice addition to dinner." He said. "I brought a fishin' pole and some flies."

It was still early when we crawled in our bags and as we lay there Terry and I urged Rex to tell us about his years working on ranches. He said he started cowboying in Arizona where he was raised. Every now and again a new cowboy would be hired with stories of some other ranch in beautiful country that paid better. Eventually he couldn't resist and headed off to greener pastures. He worked on ranches in southern Nevada usually staying a year or two until the itch to move would get him. He slowly worked his way north into northern Nevada and eastern Oregon working on ranches for a few years then moving on. It was the lifestyle that many cowboys of that era lived. He was presently working on a large ranch in Nevada, near the Oregon border. He liked it there and had stayed 5 years; longer than any job he had ever had. For a couple of young men like Terry and I just out of our childhood days of playing cowboy, his lifestyle and tales were fodder for our dreams.

Rex said occasionally his crew would get a few days off and most of them would head for the town of Watsonville, Nevada where there were bars, gambling and whorehouses nearby. It was part of the cowboy life. He told us about Kelly, his favorite whore. Before heading to town he would call Kelly and she would reserve a whole night for him. It cost him a "pretty penny" but she was worth it "because she sure knew how to please a man." Then he went into details.

In 1956 there was no internet, movies wouldn't touch sexual subjects and the word "porn" hadn't been invented. Such things were never brought up in polite conversation. Terry had been brought up in a religious family and I was raised by my mom. There was no father-figure in my life. As a result, both of us were pretty naïve.

The things Rex was so casually talking about were both taboo and fascinating, and Terry and I were all ears as we learned about the wonders of womanhood to the glow of a fading fire.

Rex finally said, "Ya know, I been thinking about marrying Kelly and taking her to the ranch with me. I really like that gal. But I don't know. My roamin' ain't very conducive to marriage and I probably ain't done roamin'."

With that Rex began to drift off. It was beyond my imagination that anyone would want to marry a whore. I was puzzled by that, but then I wasn't a cowboy.

Soon I could hear Terry and Rex snoring. As I lay there I could see the dark shapes of horses grazing peacefully in the meadow as stars silently crossed the dark blue night sky. I didn't want to go to sleep. This whole day, this whole trip was my dream come true. I never wanted it to end.

I awoke with a start to the crackling of a roaring fire. In the gray light of dawn I could see Rex sitting on our log drinking a cup of coffee. Terry woke about the same time and we hurriedly dressed, grabbed our socks and boots heading barefoot towards the warmth of the fire. After getting our boots on and a cup of hot camp coffee down Rex started breakfast. Terry and I kept him supplied with whatever he needed; frying pan, potatoes, bacon etc. It was obvious that Rex had cooked over an open fire many times. He was a master at it. Soon we were eating crisp bacon, fried taters and eggs cooked the way we ordered.

After cleaning up we packed Betsy's packs and our saddle bags then captured the horses and led them to camp where we saddled them and loaded Betsy's packs. With Rex in the lead we began our trip to the Royal Gorge. The trail went down at an easy grade through a forest of red firs. The first few miles were uneventful. A few limbs and some small downed trees littered the trail but unlike the day before we could ride our horses.

We came to a large, ancient tree. The original trail went to the left of the tree, but years before a large log fell over the trail abutting the tree. Hikers and horsemen started going around the right side of the tree and a brushy, rough, makeshift trail came into use. Previous trail crews avoided cutting the large log out but Rex decided to open the original trail as it had a better trail surface and grade.

We dismounted and began the formidable job. Betsy wanted to wander away from Jerry and her lead rope dropped to the ground. I was continuously going back to tend to my charges and it was getting frustrating. Our chainsaw wasn't big enough to cut all the way through the log so we had to cut out large blocks from both sides then roll them down the hill. As we worked we looked ahead about 150 feet and saw another good-size log across the trail. We would be here a while.

After an hour we rolled out the last block and smoothed the trail surface with shovel and hoe. Rex and Terry grabbed their reins and began walking up to the next log with tools in hand. I mounted Jerry and began leading Betsy left around the tree on the newly cleared trail, but Betsy wanted to go right on the makeshift trail. No amount of urging on my part could get Betsy to change her mind. She had been that way before and to her it was the right way; the only way to go! I mentioned before about a horses memory and I was getting example of it. I finally gave up and gave Betsy some rope so she could lead me and Jerry her way.

We took a break before starting the next log. While smoking our cigarette Betsy moved away from Jerry and once more her lead rope dropped to the ground. I retrieved her, and totally disgusted with the situation, I gave Betsy about 20 feet of rope and tied a lose knot around Jerry's saddle horn. I figured that as she ambled away she would feel a little tension on her rope and stop. I walked back to the crew just as Terry started up the chainsaw. All hell broke loose!

Jerry bolted and began running back the way we had come. When he got to the end of my 20 feet of rope my loose knot didn't slip as I had calculated; it tightened! Jerry was knocked to his front knees, and the strong pull on Betsy's halter spooked her. She began following Jerry at a full run; the rope still attached to both horses. By the time she reached Jerry he was up and running again. Then they came to the ancient tree! Jerry went right on the newly cleared trail and Betsy went left, the way she knew. The rope went around the tree. I watched in total terror as the inevitable happened. They reached the end of their rope!

Betsy was knocked on her side and immediately began pawing air to get up. Meanwhile, the rope jerked Jerry back and he reared up, spinning in the air and coming to earth facing the way he had just came. He whirled and started running back up the trail pulling Betsy around the tree as she struggled to get to her feet. When she finally made it up she was on the newly cleared trail and both totally spooked horses ran away at full speed. Betsy's pack-saddle had slipped to one side in the melee. We watched in horror as pots and pans, bottles and cans, and assorted camping gear was strewn on the ground until the horses galloped out of sight.

We weren't fast enough to prevent the disaster and no one had spoken during it. There was a long silence afterward until I asked. "What made Jerry spook?"

"Dunno,' maybe a bee stung him. Never know what might happen." Rex said. "How'd we get a knot in that rope?" He asked, looking at me. I sheepishly told him what I had done then weakly added "It was a loose knot; I thought it would slip out."

He glared at me and growled, "Told ya not to do that!" Then he went into action. "You boys walk up the trail and gather up our gear in piles. Keep Romper tied up so he doesn't try to follow me. Keep a close watch on him; we don't need another lost horse. I'm gonna' follow 'em back and see if I can round 'em up." He mounted Midnight and started up the trail at a gallop.

Terry and I worked a couple hundred feet back up the trail, searching carefully and gathering up our goods in a pile. Then Terry would go back and lead Romper up near us so we could keep an eye on him. We repeated the process for about a half-mile and began running out of things to pick up, so we sat down by the trail and took a break.

"I just don't understand why Jerry ran; he's never done that before." I offered.

"I don't know," Terry said, "Maybe when the chainsaw started he saw some movement like a twig falling or the wind blowing. Guess we'll never know."

We were about ready to continue up the trail when we saw Rex coming; leading Betsy and Jerry. "Well, they was right where I figured they'd be. Back at the meadow grazing peacefully. Had no trouble rounding 'em up. Betsy's pack-saddle was under her belly and Jerry's saddle was cockeyed; the rope slipped off his saddle horn. The good thing is neither horse got injured. Betsy's packs slipped off the pack-saddle horns and I found both of 'em in the trail. There was still some stuff in 'em and I picked up a few other things on the trail. You guys got the rest of it? Here's your horse Lloyd." He said while handing me Jerry's reins.

I mounted Jerry and grabbed Betsy's lead rope and we headed back down the trail picking up piles as we went. Back at the log we tied all the horses to trees and Rex had Terry start cutting blocks off. None of the horses blinked an eye when the chainsaw roared to life.

Rex and I took the packs off Betsy and repacked everything in the bags. It seemed we hadn't lost a thing and nothing was broken. We'd had our eggs wrapped in the ground tarp and not one had so much as a crack. Except for a lot of ruckus and a couple of lost hours everything was back to normal. I was lucky! Once done we helped Terry roll the blocks out and soon the trail was clear.

A short way further we came to a small grassy glade where the trail turned abruptly south down a steep grade. It was the beginning of the decent into the Royal Gorge. Rex pulled to a stop, dismounted and said, "Had a change of plans. It's pretty rough going down there; steep with cliffs on both sides and lots of switchbacks. We don't need to take Betsy with her heavy packs down. Terry and I will work the trail. Lloyd, you stay here with Betsy and Jerry and let them graze and we'll be back in a couple hours. We'll camp back at the meadow."

He pulled a halter and rope out and said, "Put this on Jerry 'til we get back." With the chainsaw securely tied behind Terry's saddle they started down the trail. Leaving me alone.

I got the horses situated, took a seat on a rock and lit up a cigarette. Damn! I'd really screwed things up by putting a knot in that rope. I knew Rex didn't want me on that steep trail because he didn't trust me after my blunder. You could lose more than a few things on the trail down there. You could lose a horse! Rex didn't want to take a chance with me. I screwed up Rex's chance to camp at his favorite spot, and his chance to go fishing. I screwed up my chance to see the beauty of the Royal Gorge. I screwed up everything! I wondered about my future. Would Rex kick me off the crew when we got back to Big Bend? Would I get fired? By the time Rex and Terry got back I'd beat myself up pretty good and I was one sad and sorry lad!

They were back in a couple of hours and told me the work was pretty easy; just a few boulders and limbs in the trail and no logs. The ride back to the meadow was quiet. We got the horses out to pasture and camp set up quickly since we had learned what we were doing the day before. Then we gathered around the fire with our coffee. Terry wandered off into the woods to answer natures call and that left just me and Rex. I gathered up all the courage I could and said, "Rex, I'm really sorry about what I did down there. I just wanted to help you guys. Sorry!"

Rex gazed at me for what seemed like forever and said, "Ah, don't lose no sleep over it. They always told me if you don't make no mistakes you ain't doin' nothing and I made lots of them when I was learnin'. Some was worse than you did today. Just remember, I been doing this a long time and if I tell you how to do something and you don't understand why, well, just ask me and I'll try and explain it." Then he offered me his hand and said, "You'll do alright Lloyd, just keep at it." With a big grin and a laugh he shook my hand. "I reckon you learned today that it's better to have one horse run off than two of 'em tied together."

I felt a whole lot better after that exchange and when Terry returned the chatter around the campfire returned to normal.

We were up early the next morning and left our camp in place as we started off to work a trail that went west about 5 miles. We would return to the meadow to camp on our last evening. The trail took us past Devils Peak, an unusual peak for the Sierras. Most of the Sierras in this area were made of light colored granite rocks, but Devils Peak was dark colored columns of volcanic basalt.

It was an easy trail to maintain and our work went smoothly. My blunder of the preceding day was forgotten and all was normal.

We were back at camp by 3 o'clock and Terry and I went for another bareback ride. This time I rode Jerry, and Jerry did jump the creek.

On our last day we packed up camp and worked our way down to Big Bend. After tending to our gear and horses our day was over. Rex would be gone for a few days. He was going to take Prince back to the ranch and spend a few days there before we did any more trail work.

The rest of the summer was uneventful We worked a few more trails with Rex and when we weren't on trail-duty Terry and I maintained campgrounds and worked on some of the buildings around the Ranger Station. Rex went home to the ranch sometime in mid-August taking all the horses except Betsy with him. Betsy was transported to her winter quarters on a ranch in the foothills. Terry and I were laid off in early September. The next year I got a job as a lookout in Oregon and I lost track of Terry and Rex. I haven't seen them since.

SOME AFTERTHOUGHTS

After our rescue mission I never heard how Sarah made it back to San Francisco or what the outcome with John was. I assume that Sarah caught a Greyhound Bus since the company had a stop at Soda Springs. I wonder what stories John told his wife in San Francisco?

It's funny how memories work. I spent a whole summer working trails at Big Bend but only a few of my experiences come back to me crystal clear. I suppose it's those memories that are most eventful. For an 18-year-old kid it was exciting to be on a rescue mission in the High Sierras and those memories stick with me.

I remember well our first 4-day trail trip. I can still see in slow-motion clarity Jerry going around the right side of that tree and Betsy going to the left, and I feel the same horror every time I visualize it. I clearly recall the happy memories of our bareback rides, and Rex telling Terry and me about his cowboy days around the campfire as we lay in in our sleeping bags. And I remember

Betsy. What a wonderful horse and companion she was. That whole trip is as if it happened yesterday.

I'm sure that Rex is dead and buried now. That day by the campfire I was vulnerable and with a few choice words he could have destroyed what little was left of my self-esteem. Instead he chose to build me up and treat my mistake as a joke that I could learn from. For that I am forever grateful. To Rex and all of those like him who have given me a second chance on my journey through life I say: Thank You!

Bessie and Me
Ramblings of a Lookout

FOREWARD

This is a brief history of my first summer in Butte Falls, Oregon as a fire lookout for the U.S. Forest Service. It details how I landed in Butte Falls from Grass Valley, California and a few of the experiences I had once I got here and started working as a fire lookout on Bessie Rock Lookout.

BUTTE FALLS

I loved the mountains and forest and after my time at Big Bend I decided I wanted a career with the Forest Service. I had visions of going to college and getting a degree in forestry. Oregon State College had the best forestry school in the Nation at the time, and to avoid paying out-of-state tuition I wanted to get residency in Oregon. During that winter at home I wrote to 15 Forest Service Ranger stations in Oregon with a job request. Thirteen of them offered me a job, mostly as a fire lookout or on the trail crew. I decided to accept the one that went to work the earliest; a fire lookout job on the Butte Falls Ranger District of the Rogue River National Forest. And that is how fate landed me in Butte Falls.

On April 7th 1957 I boarded a Greyhound bus in Grass Valley, California bound for Medford, Oregon; I was 19 years old.

Greyhounds then had no air conditioning and it was a hot day. Everyone in the bus was suffering from the heat and humidity on the 10-hour trip (Interstate 5 didn't exist). The passengers were sullen and no one was chatting. As we crossed Siskiyou Pass and started down through the forest of Oregon it suddenly cooled dramatically. Everyone sighed in relief. Passengers began talking with their neighbors. A lady beside me remarked, "It's always so much nicer when you get to Oregon." That was my introduction to Oregon. It would become my home.

I had a room reserved at the Medford Hotel, and with luggage in hand I walked from the bus depot to check in. I passed time walking around Medford and eating dinner at a local restaurant. Later I called my mom and told her I had landed safely in Oregon, then went to bed.

Up early the next morning I ate breakfast at the hotel, then stepped outside and stood at the hotel entrance waiting for the ride that the Butte Fall Ranger Station promised me would be there. Around 9:00, a burly fellow showed up in a familiar green Forest Service pickup. It was Claude Curtis. As we rode to Butte Falls Claude pointed out the sites. Going through Agate Desert (now called White City) Claude pointed to a snow-capped Mount Pit (McLoughlin) and said, "That's where we're going." I was thrilled. I had grown up in the Sierras of California and loved high mountains and wilderness.

In 1957 White City did not exist. Between Medford (which ended where the freeways is now) and Eagle Point there was one tavern, one gas station, the Veterans Hospital, and a half-dozen or so small farms.

After the hour trip we arrived at the Butte Falls Ranger Station and I was shown my quarters. I would start work the next day so I had the rest of the day to acquaint myself with the tiny village of Butte Falls. I found the post office at the hardware store and was issued P.O. Box 3. I still have it 56 years later.

I was hired for a fire lookout job, but since the lookout wasn't staffed until mid-June they put me to work on a field crew until the lookout was snow-free. I planted, pruned and thinned trees, piled brush, cleared trails and repaired phone lines. I stayed in the small one-room shack that was the crew quarters located at the Ranger Station. During my time at Butte Falls I made lifelong friends. One evening I ate dinner at the Butte Falls Cafe and met a young girl who was my waitress. Somewhere in our conversation she offered to wash my clothes. We agreed on a price and as time passed our relationship grew. Linda Hawkins would eventually become my wife.

Nicknames were a big thing on the crew. All of the fellows were much older than me and had lived around Butte Falls most of their lives. They decided I needed a nickname. There was one very tall, skinny fellow on the crew named Lloyd Mcloughlin and his nickname was "Mt Pit." Since my name was Lloyd too, and since I was shorter than him, they called me "Little Pit." Newcomers stood out in the very small town of Butte Falls and most of the town's folk knew me only by sight. For the first year I was known by many simply as, "That kid from California."

I became familiar with the people at the Forest Service while working on the crew. All of that would help me when I finally went to Bessie Rock as a naïve 19-year-old.

MY INTRODUCTION TO BESSIE

The Scotty alarm clock woke me at 5AM. I made coffee and ate a quick breakfast then strolled over to the warehouse where the supplies for my stay on Bessie Rock Lookout were stored. I waited for Claude Curtis to bring the pickup that would carry me and my supplies to Lodgepole Guard Station where I would meet Gordon Walker and the mules that would carry my supplies to the lookout. It was June 15, 1957. I was an excited 19-year-old kid from California and it was a beautiful spring day.

Claude came with the pickup. I knew Claude well by then. He was always in a good mood and was quick to grin; a good traveling companion. We loaded my gear and began the 45-minute drive in the early light of dawn. The Prospect and Lodgepole roads were gravel in those days and a swirl of dust followed us as we drove deeper and deeper into the forest. Finally, we came to the big meadow, barn and cabin that were Lodgepole Guard Station.

We pulled up to the barn where Gordon was already loading the horse and mules. With everything loaded in the stock truck, including my supplies, we waved goodbye to Claude and started off on the hour drive to Bessie Creek Shelter. The shelter is a typical lean-to type log and shake structure built by the CCC during the 30's. The Forest Service had built many of these in remote areas as emergency shelter for horsemen and hikers. This one was at the end of the road on headwaters of Bessie Creek. From here on it was wilderness.

I had worked with Gordon earlier repairing phone lines. He was a gentle quiet man with a ready smile and a good sense of humor. During the many years I would know him I never heard him raise his voice in anger. He's one of the few men I have met I can call a true gentleman. Gordon was a master with animals and it was a pleasure to watch him unload and handle the horse and mules. He walked and talked slow as he moved around the animals. He kept a hand on them and spoke in low tones so they always knew where he was and what he was doing. He had packed men and supplies into the backcountry for years and had learned all of the tricks, and so had the mules. They trusted him. I was his "gofer" as he saddled the animals and packed my supplies in packs which he carefully balanced. Included in the load was 20 gallons of water, two 5-gallon propane tanks and some hay for the horse and the mules. Gordon bragged that he had never broke an egg and I sure hoped so, because I had brought several dozen.

It was around 9:30 AM when Gordon climbed aboard his saddle and led the pack string through the meadow to Bessie Rock trail. I followed the string on foot, happy to be on the way to my summer home. The trail began to climb and it was all uphill through a dense Shasta-fir forest. The high altitude air was refreshing, scented with the aroma of the forest. Near the top we ran into large, late spring snowdrifts which the mules crossed with ease. After 4 miles and one last switchback in the trail, Bessie Rock came into view. It was an impressive sight. My new home was 100 feet in the air!

We unloaded packs and loosened the saddle straps on the animals, then fed them some hay. Gordon began introducing me to my new summer home. In the timber a few hundred feet southwest of the rock sat the outhouse that would be my bathroom. Near it was the garbage pit where all of the garbage accumulated by the lookout was disposed. Leftover food, cans, bottles, dead batteries, everything went in. Environmentalist would throw their hands up in horror if they saw the same thing today, but then it was a perfectly acceptable and very adequate way to treat garbage. Such pits were common throughout the National Forest at guard stations and campgrounds; and at the isolated ranches that bordered the Forests. Like most, this one had a heavy bear-proof wooden cover over the pit with a small trap door that was lifted to throw the garbage in. When the pit was full a new pit was dug nearby and the old pit was covered with soil and rocks. Ah, the good old days!

It was time to climb the rock and open the lookout for the summer. Bessie Rock is actually two rocks; the core of an ancient volcano. The cone of the volcano eroded away and left behind the hard magma vent that once spewed lava from the top of the mountain. Freezing and thawing had split the vent. The western half leaned slightly westward, while the eastern rock rose straight up over 100 feet on the south side and several hundred feet on the north side. The lookout sat on top of that spire. When the lookout was built in 1931 a series of wooden ladders bolted to the rock gave access to the cabin. A few years before I got there it was replaced with an aluminum ladder that had safety belts attached to a third rail that ran up the middle. Remnants of the old wooden ladder were still visible. As a young lad with no fear of heights, I was looking forward to the climb.

The Forest Service was a safety conscious outfit. Gordon explained that I was expected to always use the safety belts while I was lookout. I strapped on my belt and followed Gordon up the rock. The safety belts were built so they slid up and down the ladder as long as no tension was placed on them. If you put tension on them a locking mechanism kicked in and you couldn't fall far. It was a safe system but climbing the ladder with your belt attached to the rail was a bit cumbersome.

The climb was exhilarating. More and more of the surrounding country came into view as we neared the top. When I made the last few steps I saw my summer home. Once up, we took a breather and ate our lunch. I smoked a cigarette and surveyed the terrain. To my south were dense forests and the deep canyon of the Middle Fork of the Rogue River, and to my west, rolling timber-covered mountains. To my north I saw the deep canyon of Red Blanket Creek and more rolling mountains of timber, and to the east sat the high peaks of the Cascade Mountains crest. It was an awesome view and one that I was fortunate to live with daily.

Our first job was to open the lookout. We loosened the shutters that had been bolted down the previous fall. We swung them up and braced them in place with struts. We did this on all four sides exposing the windows that were the walls of the lookout. Then we unlocked the door and stepped in. The building had survived the harsh winter wind and snow in good shape, except for the damage the mice did. I have forever been amazed at how tiny mice scale that high steep rock. But there, right in front of me was the proof. Mouse droppings littered the floor and scraps of paper were strewn about. They used the paper to line their nest. But how they got there and how they survive during the long winter is a mystery to me. One of my first jobs would be trapping mice. They're not good companions in a small cabin.

We inspected cabinets and drawers, then began dusting and sweeping the mouse mess. An hour later my home was ship-shape. Now the big job: Getting supplies up to the top. Gordon showed me how to operate the davit crane. This was a hand cranked crane that swung out over the edge of the rock. Then a rope with a hook attached was lowered to the ground when the brake was released. When Gordon was sufficiently satisfied I could operate it safely he went to the ground and prepared loads for me to hoist up. I cranked the loads up, swung them over the rock, unhooked them and the whole process started over. It took about eight loads to get everything up; batteries, propane, water cans, my personal gear and assorted lookout tools.

Once done, Gordon joined me and we put everything in its place. We hooked up the propane and Gordon showed me how to light the pilot lights on my gas range, refrigerator, heater, and how to operate the gas lamp. I temporarily stowed my personal gear and food that I would rearrange later to make it more convenient. One water can and the extra propane tank went out on the catwalk. It was time to make the lookout functional.

Bessie had two means of communication with the outside world. When the lookout was first built a telephone line was put in from the lookout to Imnaha Guard Station. From there it went to Lodgepole Guard Station and on to the Butte Falls Ranger Station. The system was hooked up to every lookout and guard station on the District. It was a local system. It wasn't possible to call phones that weren't on it. In those early days it was the only communications. The line was still in place and maintained, but two-way radios had become the preferred communication system. In 1957, two-way radios were not as dependable as they are now and the phone was used as backup if the two-way radio failed. It was an old fashion crank phone. Gordon gave it three quick cranks and began talking to the dispatcher, Suzie, at Butte Falls. Looking at me with a smile on his face he explained to Suzie that we were almost done opening the lookout and that the 'Kid from California' just might make an OK lookout. The phone was operational and it felt good that Gordon had given me a vote of confidence. Everyone admired his judgment and a pat on the back from Gordon was gold.

We placed the lookout's two-way radio on a small table. Portable radios then were partly transistor and partly tube and used more power than those of today. Beneath the table we put a box with a dozen large 1.5 volt batteries and hooked them up to the radio. These batteries were about eight inches tall and as big around as a coffee cup. I would have to change the batteries three times before the summer was over. The antenna on the roof was connected and the radio turned on. Gordon took the mike and called the Ranger Station:

"Butte Falls, this is Bessie. Radio check?"

"10-4 Bessie, we have a strong signal here. Looks like everything is working."

"Thanks Suzie, and Bessie is now open for business. Bessie Rock is 10-8."

In the 10 code, 10-8 means the station is currently on the air. Bessie Rock was officially open and I was happy to be there.

For the remainder of Gordon's time he gave me technical instructions. I had already had some training with the Osborne Fire Finder and map reading, so he concentrated on showing me local landmarks. From our perch we could see other lookouts, Rustler Peak to the south, Blue Rock to the southeast, Devils Peak on the crest of the Cascade Mountains, Fredenburg Butte to the southwest near Butte Falls, and Halls Point northwest on the Prospect Ranger District. He pointed out several rock slides on distant ridges and pretending they were actual fires I went through the process of preparing a fire report.

Around 3:30 p.m. Gordon still had a long day left. He told me goodbye and headed down the ladder. It would be around 7 p.m. before he was at Lodgepole with the animals unloaded and fed, and the saddles and packs stowed away. I went to the edge of the rock and watched as he saddled the horse and mules. He swung to the saddle and with a farewell wave headed down the trail. With one more wave and a big grin, he rounded a corner and disappeared from my sight. I would not see Gordon again for 2 weeks, when he would return to re-supply me. As much as I liked Gordon and his company, I was glad he was gone. I was now alone and in charge of the lookout; my first day on Bessie Rock.

I went back in the lookout to rearrange my personal gear, stow all my food and inspect what kind of cooking and eating utensils I had. I had plenty including a large pan that would double for dishes and sponge baths. I had coffee cups, glasses, plates, bowls and silverware. There was a spatula and several large mixing spoons. I was happy to see a couple of cake pans and a cookie sheet because I had brought the makings.

The fridge was small, like those found in camp trailers and I didn't have enough room for all the fresh foods I had brought. In a small storage cellar under the lookout I found a mouse proof box that I put my fresh vegetables in. I put the veggies on the catwalk and as long as I remembered to move the box to the shady side of the lookout they would keep good in the cool mountain air. It was a good system and it worked well for the rest of my stay. Some of my meat went in the freezer compartment of the fridge, the rest in the cooling section along with milk, butter, eggs and condiments. Then I stowed my canned and dry goods, along with paper plates I had brought. The lookout was stocked with porcelain plates. I had no use for the paper ones, but I would later find a very interesting use for them.

THE ROCK AND MY HOUSE

Bessie Rock is right at 6,000 feet elevation, and as I have said it's actually two rocks. The spire that the building sat on was slightly rounded on top and the lookout sat on the highest part. As I recall there was about 30 feet of space on each side of the lookout where you could walk or lounge without fear of getting too close to the edge. Beyond that it was dangerous since the rock dropped off abruptly and then it was vertical all the way to the rocky ground below.

The north side had the most breathtaking view and you could walk close to the edge. Below was the spectacular canyon of Red Blanket Creek. The creek was 1,600 vertical feet below the lookout. Bessie Rock dropped straight down about 200 feet to a rocky slope that fell off at a steep angle 500 feet further. Below that were the steep timbered slopes of the canyon. It was an awe-inspiring sight.

Bessie Rock was a standard Forest Service L-4 lookout cabin with a peaked roof and a 4-foot-wide catwalk surrounding the cabin. A lighting rod was attached at the top of the peak with four cable leads going to the ground. Each of these cables was buried 2 feet deep for 100 feet out into the forest below to provide a good electrical ground. The building was 14 feet by 14 feet with a 7-foot ceiling. The walls were wood up about 2 feet from the floor then paned glass window to the ceiling.

It had a single bed that was made for lightning protection. A wooden frame was mounted on glass telephone insulators. Ropes stretched tightly between the frame substituted for metal springs and the mattress lay on top. The Osborne Fire Finder sat in the center of the room on a stand 2 feet by 2 feet and 4 feet high. A glass insulated stool sat next to the stand. On the north side was a 2-foot high desk with drawers and cupboards underneath. On the east were kitchen cupboards also 2 feet high, and counter tops along with the gas range, and fridge. There was one office chair mounted on wheels. Everything was designed to be 2 feet high to not block the view from inside the lookout. The gas range and fridge at 3 feet high were the exceptions. My home was sparsely furnished but did the job.

Bessie Rock Lookout.
The wood ladder was in place
when Photo was shot.

The Wood Ladder
The new ladder was at a new location
about 40 feet away.

Bessie Lookout Cabin.
There's nothing quite as ugly as an lookout with its shutters down.
When their up its an elegant looking building.

BESSIE ROCK FLOOR PLAN

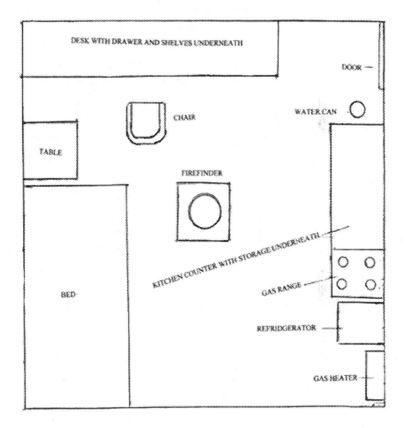

A Day in the Life of a Lookout

There is nothing like daybreak on a lookout! High in the mountains above the valley mist the air is crystal clear. As the sun first breaks over the eastern ridge it seems that everything sparkles! It's impossible for words like sad, blue, or depressed to be part of your vocabulary. Each morning is a spiritual moment, and unforgettable. I loved my mornings on Bessie.

I usually woke at daybreak and watched the sunrise from bed as I cleared the sleepiness. Once dressed, I walked the catwalk inspecting the mountains before me. If necessary I took a trip to the ground to use the outhouse. Back on top I made coffee, and often stepped outside in the cool air to find a seat on the rocks where I drank my coffee, and smoked my first cigarette. I took in the surrounding country looking for anything out of the ordinary. Back inside I turned the Forest Service radio on to listen to any morning chatter and began cooking my breakfast.

As strange as it may sound, one of the hottest times of the day inside a lookout is in the cool early morning. That's because a lookout is essentially a hothouse; a small building with glass walls. Once the sun rises and until it moves above the shutters the sunlight pours directly into the windows of the building and quickly heats the interior to uncomfortable temperatures. To combat the rising temperatures I opened the door and a window to let the cool morning air circulate.

When I was 6 years old my father got tired of marriage and just took off one day. My mother raised three boys alone. She had to work, so we learned to fend for ourselves. For many years we got up and made our own breakfast and packed our school lunch. Many evenings we cooked our own supper. Cooking did not intimidate me. As a result, I seldom ate canned or prepackage meals as many other the lookouts did. I ate home-cooked meals. My breakfasts were usually bacon, eggs over easy, with hash browns; or pancakes and eggs. I rarely ate dried breakfast food like corn flakes. I always washed dishes immediately after. It's a habit I got as a kid. It's easier to clean dishes if dried food isn't stuck to them.

After breakfast I officially signed on the radio, letting the world know that Bessie Rock was open and operational. I would key the mike and say, "Butte Falls, Bessie Rock is 10-8." It was usually around 6 or 7 a.m. Once done the entire Rogue River National Forest knew I was operational. My official hours were 9 a.m. to 6 p.m., and that's the hours I was paid for, but all lookouts know that you are on duty 24 hours a day. It's impossible not to be when your work place is your home.

A little about radio use: Forest Service radios were strictly for business and all messages were to be kept short so as not to tie up the air waves. The entire Rogue River National Forest was on the same frequency. No personal use was allowed at any time. It was the same with the phone with one exception. After 7 p.m. lookouts were allowed to chat with other lookouts or guard stations if they were lonely and needed to hear a human voice. I seldom used that privilege because I seldom got lonely.

Lookouts were expected to go outside every 15 minute and slowly walk around the catwalk searching the mountains and canyons for wisps of smoke that may be a forest fire. My first few days I did that, but it soon became apparent the walk-around was not necessary. Once you became accustomed to your surroundings it became second nature to scan it at all times. It could be done from inside or outside the lookout with equal effectiveness. You automatically became keenly aware of anything that didn't look right. So on most days I made the walk around the catwalk only when I wanted to stretch my legs and get a breath of fresh mountain air.

I had methods to fight boredom. In the mornings I spent several hours learning the country. I created fires in my mind then tried to locate them. A rock wall on a faraway ridge became a dangerous fire. I spent time getting an azimuth and vertical angle, both of which were easy. Then I had to get a distance, and that was difficult. By drawing out the azimuth on a topographic map you could get close, or so I hoped. Then I'd give a legal description; Township 34 south, Range 3 east; the north east, of the southeast quarter of section 16! Every day on Bessie I practiced for the actual few minutes that I would need those skills. In the end all of that practice paid off.

Washing windows was morning job. The outsides of the windows did not need cleaning often. But the gas stove created a film on the inside and they needed cleaning at least once a week. There were five windows on a side and each had 6 panes. Totals to about 90 single panes! I did half the lookout one day, and the other half at a later day, so I didn't have to do the whole job at once.

Occasionally I needed to wash clothes, usually under garments. Being a lookout was not a dirty job so I only washed the heavy pants and shirts when I made it back to Butte Falls. Washing socks, T-shirts and underwear was a problem since I had limited water. Washing is the wrong word since I used no soap. With as little hot water as possible I rinsed and wrung them out. Someone before me had strung a clothes line on the ceiling that was handy for drying.

I was an avid reader and brought books with me. I read about 15 minutes, scanned the forest around me, and then read another 15 minutes. I brought crossword books and had a deck of cards for solitaire. And I had my portable (commercial) radio.

The radio was a 19-year-olds' savior! I tuned it to the local Rock and Roll stations during the day. KBOY out of Medford was one of my favorite stations. I listen to the news and weather, then to music; Elvis, Fats Domino, Little Richard. I practiced dancing to the tunes. That must have been a sight to behold! A madman dancing alone on the top of a mountain! I'm real glad that I was miles away from anybody!

The portable radios of those days were not like todays. Mine would only last a day or so on D batteries so I came up with a solution. I found some wire and hooked up several of those big Forest Service batteries to it. They lasted weeks and if I was prudent I could have all of the music I wanted

I spent a lot of time exercising. Sometimes going up and down the ladder several times just to keep in shape. Before going down I called Butte Falls and said, "Bessie is 10-7 for 15 minutes." The 10-7 meant I was out of service, which usually meant that I was going to the ground to use the outhouse. But mostly I was just stretching my legs and getting away from the lookout. I thought I was being sneaky, but in fact, most of the people in hearing range of my radio were totally aware of what I was doing and didn't blame me a bit.

I confess that I gave up using the ladders safety belts on my first day alone on the mountain. As a kid I loved to climb trees and had no fear of heights, and the rungs of a ladder were easy compared to the slick barked limbs of a tree. Besides, dealing with the belt was a nuisance. The only time I used it was if another Forest Service person was around, or when it rained or snowed. I was young, dumb and happy. I never made it public that I didn't use the belts. Had Doug Finch, the Fire Control Officer in Butte Falls found out I would have lost my job.

Around noon I ate lunch. Lunch was the one meal that I did eat canned foods on a regular basis. Usually a bowl of Campbell's soup and some fruit or sandwich. I often made lemonade or Kool-Aid to go along with my meal. There was no faucet on Bessie. I dipped water from the milk cans for the lemonade, and heated it on the stove for dishes or baths. You had to be careful with water. You only had about 10 gallons a week for all your uses.

Afternoons was when I did much of my pleasure reading and studying Forest Service manuals. I had manuals for lookouts, fire behavior and weather. As a kid I was always interested in weather. Getting my first thermometer was as great as getting my first bike and I started keeping a record of high and low temperatures. The Forest Service weather manual had explanations of high and low pressure systems and lessons on the behavior of wind, as well as pictures of the various cloud types and what they mean for future weather. Since I was a weather nut it was all interesting reading for me. A lookout is a great place to study weather because of the view of the sky you get.

I spent a lot of time on the catwalk afternoons. I took my chair outside and read while occasionally scanning the country around me. And then there was one of my favorite pastimes. Flying paper airplanes off the rock! I started designing paper planes with the goal of finding a design that would drift over the deep canyon of Red Blanket Creek for a long time. I went to the north side of the rock overlooking the canyon to launch them. It took me a while to find the best design for sustained flights, and when I did, it was the simplest, one we all made in grade school. It had a small body, lots of wing space and a sharp, light nose. In the afternoons updrafts were created by warm air rising out of the canyon. On a good day I could launch a plane and watch it sail, sometimes even rise, for more than a half hour until it finally got so far away I lost sight of it. Then I got a bright idea and started writing notes on them like, "Help! I'm being held captive!" I still wonder if some fisherman on Red Blanket Creek ever found one. Ah youth!

Watching hawks was great entertainment. In the afternoon when the updrafts were in effect red-tail hawks gathered over Bessie and soared to great heights then glided down the ridge-tops seeking prey. But their most impressive display was during mating season. A couple of hawks gained altitude over Bessie, then would glide north over Red Blanket Canyon and at some point determined by the hawks, they suddenly folded their wings and dove straight down, gaining speed and hurling uncontrolled; 100 feet, 200 feet, as much as 400 feet straight down. Then they would extend their wings, make a graceful arch and shoot skyward carried by the momentum they gained in the dive. At the top of the climb they extended their wings and circled, gaining altitude over Bessie so they could repeat the whole thing again. I understand it's a mating ritual where each hawk tries to impress the other with its aerial skills and agility. I know I was impressed and I spent hours watching hawks.

Except for birds there wasn't much wildlife to observe from Bessie. The dense Shasta-fir forest closed in on the base of the rock on three sides and all I could see was the tops of trees. There was one small clear area on the south side where the trail was located, but except for some deer I saw few animals. Occasionally in the evening I went to the ground and walked the trail a mile or so for exercise. I often saw wildlife tracks; deer, elk, coyote, bear and mountain lions were all residents. I often heard the coyotes howling after dark and I once saw a momma bear and her cubs on the trail.

I loved to cloud watch. Most lookouts do. We would often get a weather forecast for possible thunderstorms. On those days cumulus clouds would begin to build over the mountains around 1 p.m. and lookouts would eagerly look forward to a good storm. We were on our posts for a reason. We had honed our skills and wanted to use them. We watched the clouds and rooted for them to develop into full-fledged thunderstorms.

It didn't take long for me to discover that in mountainous areas, cumulus clouds developed in the same areas over and over. I named the clouds. The Mt. Pit Cloud developed northeast of the mountain, the Fredenburgh Cloud developed northeast of Fredenburgh Butte and the Crater Lake cloud developed over the high ridges surrounding the north and east side of the lake, and there were others.

Weathermen recognize three stages of thunderstorm development. First there are the puffy *cumulus* clouds we all see on pleasant summer days. As the afternoon heats up, updrafts develop and the puffy clouds begin to grow taller, they are then called *towering cumulus*. A few showers begin to fall from the tallest ones. If the cloud continues to grow they will reach an altitude where there are high winds (thirty to fifty thousand feet.) The cloud doesn't grow past the altitude. Instead the prevailing winds spreads the cloud top in the direction of the wind; usually northeast in our area. That creates what is known as an anvil. The flattened cloud top created by the wind spreads northeast and it resembles a blacksmiths anvil. At this point it's a full-fledged *thunderstorm* and you usually get heavy showers, high, erratic winds, with lightning and thunder, but not always. If the humidity in the lower atmosphere is very low, the showers evaporate before they reach the ground. This is known as a dry thunderstorm and they are the most dangerous since there is no rain to dampen fires started by lightning. This was this process I watched from Bessie, along with every other fire lookout in the country. When the clouds began to tower I dropped my other activities and went into full time cloud watching mode.

I've often been told by friends that I must have got lonely while on the lookout. My answer is, with one small exception I never did. Many lookouts did, some could not take it a whole summer and requested to be relieved. Some created crisis in or around the lookout so someone from the Ranger Station would have to visit him to quell the crisis. After a couple of those episodes they were usually terminated. But I never got lonely. I viewed the mountains surrounding me, and the hawks and clouds as my friends. Bessie Rock herself as my best friend. How can one get lonely surrounded by friends? This may sound a bit fanciful but it's true. I daydreamed about my girlfriend, my future and things like that, but loneliness was never a problem.

The exception was the first week on the lookout. Whenever I sat down to eat supper, a haunting loneliness overcame me. I didn't understand it, but there it was. Then one day I figured it out. Most of us eat our suppers with family, or friends. We talk about our day, our plans, and our dreams. Rarely do we eat the evening meal alone. Even if we eat alone at a restaurant there is conversation all around us. I had that haunting lonely feeling because I was missing companions for supper! Once I understood, the loneliness disappeared.

It's a good thing loneliness wasn't a problem with me. Most lookouts get a steady stream of visitors but not Bessie Rock. We had four fulltime lookouts on our District. Rustler Peak was the main lookout. It had the most widespread vista of the District and was the main communications hub. Crews working in the forest called Rustler to relay messages to Butte Falls, and it had a road to it. Tourists, hunters and forest service people often dropped by. Only the most experienced lookouts were assigned to Rustler.

Blue Rock was near the popular Blue Canyon Trail Head and had a jeep road to it. Horsemen and backpackers often took a trip to visit the lookout at Blue Rock.

Devils Peak was the most isolated lookout. In 1957 it was a 9-mile hike in, and at 7,682 feet elevation it was the highest lookout on the Rogue River National Forest. But a half-mile northwest was Seven Lakes Basin, and a mile southwest was the Sky Lakes Basin. Both were popular backpacking, fishing and camping spots and many people, once in there, took the time to visit the lookout and take in the spectacular view.

There was nothing at Bessie Rock to entice visitors. No road, no lakes and the nearest fishing stream was 1,800 feet below in a steep canyon. The summer I was there I had exactly three visitors and they all came as one group; three horseback riders, one woman and two men. I heard the horses coming up the trail and went out to greet them. I told them it was OK if they wanted to come up and see the view, but the woman was afraid of the ladder. I went down and visited for about 10 minutes. I couldn't convince any of them to climb the ladder, even with the safety belts. After a short stay they headed back down the trail. That was the extent of my visitors for the entire summer.

As mentioned, the outhouse was on the ground. Normally this wasn't a problem. To urinate I just stepped outside and whizzed off the catwalk. But a very few times Mother Nature would give an *urgent* call to defecate and this was a problem! There just might not be enough time to safely descend that 100-foot ladder! That's when the paper plates came in handy. I'd grab a paper plate, go outside and do my duty. Then go to the north side of the rock and toss plate and all overboard. You have to be creative on a lookout!

Except for early mornings and late afternoons when the sun poured in the windows summer temperatures at that elevation were comfortable. On a very hot day in the valley it might get up to 75 degrees on Bessie; rarely 80 degrees. More often than not it was cool on the mountain and required a heavy shirt or light coat. In late afternoons the sun would again stream through the windows and heat the building up rapidly; time to open the door and windows. I usually waited until the sun went down to cook supper because the gas stove would add more heat and make it unbearable in the lookout.

Around 4 p.m. I reported my weather conditions. Bessie had a small weather station outside with a high/low thermometer, rain gauge, and wind vane and wind speed indicator. It had fuel moisture sticks. These are four round wooden dowels attached together. I weighed them and the more they weighed the more moisture was in them and vice versa. It also had what's called a wet/dry bulb with which you calculated relative humidity. It took me about 30 minutes to gather the information and record it on a weather form. I then called the Rogue River National Forest headquarters at Medford.

I read them a series of numbers which was my information. Headquarters gathered this information from every lookout, guard station and District headquarters on the Forest. They used it to calculate the Fire Hazard that was broadcast on most radio and TV station in the valley. You may have seen the signs that are located at ranger stations and at Forest boundaries:

THE FIRE HAZARD TODAY
IS MODERATE

Rogue River National Forest headquarters passed the information on to the National Weather Service located at the Medford Airport, who used it to help prepare their daily forecasts, then to the Forest Service Regional headquarters at Portland. They used it to schedule fire crews around the Northwest. An area with a low fire hazard might put their crews on alert to be sent to an area with an extreme fire hazard. In those days the Forest Service definitely kept on top of the fire situation. I was proud to be part of that and since I was a weather freak it was enjoyable work.

When the sun was about to set I began cooking my evening meal. I ate well on Bessie. A typical meal consisted of meat (steak, pork chops or chicken), potatoes with gravy, a small can of vegetables and a lettuce and tomato salad. One of my favorite meals, probably because I had it so much as a kid, was Van Camp Pork and Beans, hot dogs and hash browns.

By the time I had the meal finished and the dishes done it was dark. I relaxed while listening to my radio and kicking back with a cup of coffee and a cigarette. By then I had turned the propane lamp on, which was situated above the stove. In addition to providing light the lamp created enough heat to keep the chill off inside the cabin. Occasionally I stepped outside to view the sky. Far from any town there was no ambient light and the night sky fairly sparkled. I took in the sights until I got chilly.

After dark I sent a message to anyone still on the air. "Bessie Rock is 10-7 for the evening." Which meant Bessie was out of service. I usually went to bed early, but not to sleep. I secured the lookout, turned off the Forest Service radio and gas light, and crawled in my sleeping bag with a book and a flashlight. I read while listening to music until sleep overcame me.

THE BREAK

Sometime in mid-July the Ranger Station called me on the phone and told me I was going to get 10 days off the lookout. There were two Forestry Students from Arkansas that had jobs with the District and they wanted to give them some experience on a lookout before they returned to school in the fall. Each would get 5 days on the lookout. It was Jack Scoby and Hank Brown. Both had come to work a couple of weeks after me and worked on one of the field crews. So one day Jack showed up with a backpack full of food and his personal gear on his back and I left Bessie. Claude was waiting for me at Bessie Shelter and gave me a ride to Butte Falls where I was looking forward to seeing my new friends and Linda.

The Forest Service in those days did not pay overtime. In lieu of overtime they gave you comp (compensatory) time. Comp time accrued and you could either use it to take time off, or request a check for it when you were terminated. I had earned some hours of comp at Bessie and decided to take a few days off during my 10 days away from Bessie.

Bessie was a great way for me to save money. I had two checks waiting for me when I went to the Post Office. I decided I needed a car. Linda was living with Bill and Mary Jo Harris during the summer. She baby-sat for them days while they both worked, and she worked part time at the restaurant in the evenings. I had become friends with Bill and he offered to co-sign for a car for me. So on a Saturday we went to Medford and found a gray "48" Ford Coupe. It was the teardrop style that was popular in the forties. We kicked the tires and took it for a drive and with a $50 down payment we signed the contract and I had wheels. I had a California driver's license which would suffice until I returned to California in the fall. In those days you didn't have to have insurance, so I drove around uninsured. On my days off I drove around Butte Falls showing off my "new car" to friends and took Linda for drives when she wasn't working. Some nights we went to the drive-in movies at the Starlight in Medford. Those were happy times. I spent the remainder of my time off Bessie working on a field crew.

FIRE IN THE MOUNTAINS!

After my hiatus from the mountain I drove to Bessie Shelter with a backpack of supplies and hiked to the lookout to resume my duties. Having my car gave me some freedom. After hours I could drive to Butte Falls to visit Linda and friends.

The first time I did, I spent time playing Hearts with the boys in the Butte Falls park, Bill Irwin, Donnie Ellis and Monty Facey. Around 11 p.m. I wanted to leave but they convinced me to stay a while longer. Hearts is a four-person game and they weren't ready to quit, and they didn't have to work in the morning! So I stayed and the night wore on. It was around 1 a.m. before I hopped in my car and headed up the mountain. It was around 2:30 a.m. when I arrived at Bessie Shelter with a 4-mile hike up a pitch black trail before me. I had a Forest Service issued headlamp that I strapped around my forehead and put the batteries in my pocket. Up the trail I went at a good pace. An hour later I was climbing the 100-foot ladder in the dark. I immediately crawled in my bag and went to sleep. I managed to wake up about 8:00 the next morning. I figured it wasn't such a good idea to go to town and only did it a couple more times.

One day in early August Gordon rode up with the pack string. He had water, batteries, food, and a propane tank for me. That morning the weather forecast was for a 40% chance of lightning storms in Southern Oregon. Gordon and I went out on the catwalk and watched as cumulus clouds began to build over the higher peaks. He said, "I reckon we'll get some boomers in the next few days. I figure I'd better hightail it to Lodgepole and get ready to pack fire crews into the backcountry." He was right.

No storms developed over our Forest that day, but they developed over Crater Lake and east of the Cascades. That night I watched clouds lighting up as lightning peppered the high desert of eastern Oregon.

The next morning the weather forecast in southwest Oregon was for an 80% chance of thunderstormswith the possibility of some dry lightning. A moist air mass was moving northeast from the Gulf of Mexico covering Nevada and skirting the Sierra Nevada Mountains. It was expected to move into southern Oregon during the day. It is that air mass that gives the Rogue River country its most intense thunderstorms and the highest chance of dry lightning.

Before I continue I need to explain how fires are located, and the mindset of people who staff the lookouts. It's usually the case that when a fire starts there is more than one lookout that can see it. When that happens, it's possible to pinpoint the location of the fire by a process called triangulation. Each lookout sends his azimuth to headquarters. They draw each azimuth on a large map. The fires location is where the lines cross. This is the most accurate method.

Sometimes only one lookout can see the fire. The lookout must get his azimuth then estimate how far along that line the fire is. If he can see the fire (flames) he can usually get pretty close by using local landmarks to help. But if the fire is out of sight in a canyon, or over a ridge, and all he can see is smoke rising, he has to estimate the distance to the fire, and that takes experience. He has to consider how dense the smoke appears and the direction the wind is drifting it. Once he estimates the distance to the fire along his azimuth, he marks it on his topographic map with a tack and gets the legal description. That information is sent to headquarters and to all concerned that's where the fire is. At least until he is proven wrong, which no lookout ever wants. Every lookout worth his salt is competitive. He wants to beat the competition and be the first to see, locate and report the fire. And he wants to do it accurately.

That morning I got my chores done early and went out on the catwalk to scan the sky. Far to my south I could see large cumulus clouds building over the Siskiyou Mountains. Around 10 p.m., clouds began popping up locally. By noon towering cumulus covered much of the area and the clouds darkened; by 2 p.m. I began hearing thunder echoing across the canyons. A few small thunderstorms were drifting northeast across the forest both north and south of me. I went in the lookout and began recording the azimuths of the ground strikes I saw. I would use them later to go back and carefully scan those areas with binoculars searching for smoke.

Before long a dark cloud rapidly spread over Bessie Rock and lightning and thunder began peppering the country around me. I took the steps I had learned to protect myself and the lookout if it took a direct lightning strike. I called Butte Falls on the radio and said, "Bessie Rock is 10-7 for the duration of the storm," then turned off the radio and disconnected it from the roof antenna. I flipped a switch that disconnected the phone. I got on the insulated stool while trying to record the lightning strikes that were all around the lookout. High winds were buffeting the lookout, rattling the shutters and door and sending hail crashing into the windows. The hail increased in size and intensity until the noise of it slamming on the windows became deafening. I could hear nothing but a constant roar. Trying to record lightning strikes became useless. There were too many coming too fast and I couldn't see them through the swirling hail. I retreated to the bed.

I had mixed emotions, I wondered if the lightning rod would perform properly if the lookout was struck. Being up near a cloud base while lightning is everywhere is a frightening experience, but at the same time it's exhilarating. My adrenalin was pumping overtime. I shuddered with excitement and fear with every loud thunder clap. Because this was my first experience with lightning on a lookout I didn't know that this is a common event that all lookouts experience at some time. Lookouts have taken direct hits, but no deaths have ever occurred.

As quickly as it came the hail turned to heavy rain, then blustery showers. The constant roar eased and the thunder faded in the distance to my northeast. The whole event had lasted only about 20 minutes.

It wasn't safe to use the radio until the storm was at least a mile away. I began estimating the distance. When I saw a flash I began counting the seconds before the thunder roared. Every 5 seconds between flash and thunder was 1 mile. When I was sure it was a mile or more distant I hooked up my radio, and turned it on, "Bessie Rock is 10-8." I immediately heard other lookouts reporting fires. Every District on the Rogue River National Forest was busy. The chatter on the radio was constant. I was anxious to report my first fire.

I put on a coat and grabbed the binoculars preparing to go out on the catwalk. Mist was drifting up from Bessie Creek canyon to my south and Red Blanket Canyon to my north. It formed a fog bank that blanketed the ridge-top where Bessie sits. I was fogged in! My visibility was cut to about 150 feet. It was maddening! I listened as both Rustler Peak and Blue Rock reported a smoke south of Rustler. Blue Rock reported another smoke near Island Lake in the back country. Gordon would be packing supplies into that one. Like me, Devils Peak reported that he was fogged in. Halls Point reported a fire on the Prospect District only a few miles northwest of Bessie. If I could see, I could get a cross azimuth and pinpoint the fire. But I was fogged in! I recorded all of the azimuths and legal descriptions reported by other lookouts in my area. It would be helpful later if I saw these smokes

The fog finally lifted and I was on the catwalk searching for smoke. I saw a tall column of smoke northwest of me that was surely the fire Halls Point had reported. I raced back inside and put the Osborne Fire Finders cross-hairs on it. I called Prospect and reported my azimuth then went back out and scanned the forest with the binoculars. Gray fog pockets were rising in the canyons imitating smoke. If I waited long enough they would dissipate and change shapes. Not smoke. Smoke is bluish gray and rises in a steady column. It doesn't dissipate; it fades away as the wind drifts it off.

I spent the afternoon searching, but found no more smoke. It's amazing that with all the lightning that struck around me that no fires started. The heavy rain and hail must have doused any that started. Around 4 p.m., Headquarters issued a special weather alert, "Large active thunderstorms have built up in Northern California and are expected to drift into Southwest Oregon during the evening hours. Expect more lightning, high winds with the possibility of some dry cells." We were going to be hit again!

Around 6 p.m. I saw a gigantic thunderstorm moving northeast over the Rogue Valley. Angry, dark cumulus clouds led the way for the black base of the storm. White clouds boiled skyward and created a well-formed anvil. This was a classic thunderstorm known by weathermen as a Super Cell. Lightning down-strikes became visible as it crossed Beekman Ridge south of Butte Falls. Soon it covered the entire District with the center passing over Rustler Peak. I was on the northern edge. I could see heavy rain falling from a 5-mile swath that was the center of the storm; from there it faded to sporadic shower. I had blustery winds but little or no rain.

I went inside the lookout and began recording the down-strikes I saw. One struck over a ridge top south of the Middle Fork. A short time later I saw a column of smoke rising from the area. I scanned it with the binoculars and saw that the smoke was rising from the far side of a ridge. The base of the fire was hidden from my view. I got an azimuth and drew a line on my topographic map.

The smoke would be visible from both Rustler Peak and Blue Rock. I looked at them and saw they were both fogged in. It was my chance to be first with a fire report! But how far over the ridge was it? That was my challenge.

Once more I went out on the catwalk with my binoculars and carefully searched, hoping I could find a landmark that I could use to get an estimated distance to the fire. Nothing! By the clarity which I could see the column I decided it had to be in an area between a quarter-mile and 1.5 miles beyond the ridge. But I was wasting time. I had to make a decision soon. I split the difference and marked the spot on my map; then measured the distance from that point to Bessie Rock, 5.6 miles. I wrote out the legal description and finished filling out the fire report form.

"Butte Falls, this is Bessie with a fire report."

"Go ahead Bessie." Suzie replied.

"Azimuth 160 degrees, 23 minutes. Vertical angle—.20 seconds. Distance to fire 5.6 miles. Location Township 33 south, Range 4 east, NW of the SW Section 12. I see a steady column of smoke but cannot see the base. I estimate the fire size at 1/10 acre."

"Ten-four Bessie. We'll get back to you."

The Forest Service understands it's not possible to always get an exact location from a single lookout. As a goal it wants all fires reported to be within a quarter-mile of the actual site. I badly wanted to meet that goal. I knew I would find out soon. When the fog cleared up on Rustler and Blue Rock they will get an azimuth to my fire and where those lines crossed mine would be the actual location. Time to pray!

A short time later I heard:

"Bessie, this is Butte Falls, The name of your fire is Imnaha Fire. A three-man crew has been dispatched. They will be going up the Alta Lake Trail until they get in the vicinity. Expect them to be arriving there in about 3 hours. What is the status of the fire now?"

"The fire is the same. Single column of smoke, not varying much." I answered.

"Ten-four Bessie, Doug wants you to stay on duty until 11 p.m.

"Ten-four, Bessie is ten-eight.

The crew would be hiking in the dark. They would arrive in the vicinity around 10 p.m. I started cooking a delayed supper when I heard Rustler report two new smokes and give an azimuth for the Imnaha Fire. I drew their azimuth on my map and it crossed mine very near the location I had given. I was ecstatic and did a little dance.

I spent the evening searching for more fires. Around 10 p.m. I heard the crew headed to my fire call Butte Falls and say they were in the area of the fire, but due to rough terrain and darkness they were going to bed down and find the fire at dawns light. Around 11 p.m. Doug called me:

"Hey kid you did an OK job, you can button it up now and be back on duty at 6 a.m."

Doug called everyone kid and getting a compliment from him was like pulling teeth. So getting an "OK job" was awesome. My first fire was a success! I went to bed happy.

The next day the crew found the fire. It was a large snag with fire in the top of it and about 1/10 acre on the ground around it. They called for a chain saw and by 4 p.m. the snag was down and the fire contained. They spent one more night there and the next day they had it dead out. It was satisfying to know I had a hand in that.

Goodbye Bessie

September was a very dry month with high fire danger. Hunting season started in October and the fire danger rose because of hunter's campfires and lots of people roaming the woods. During the early part of the month we had a few light showers but not enough rain to end fire season. About mid-October the Ranger Station pulled the Devils Peak lookout off the mountain. At its high elevation Devils Peak was prone to early heavy snows and the trail is long and treacherous. No sense getting a man trapped up there with no way to remove his gear.

Days were much cooler now and I spent more time inside. It was not uncommon for me to light the heater. I spent time baking an occasional cake, reading and walking around the catwalk to stretch my legs. They were lazy days. In the last week of the month the weatherman forecasted a major winter storm would move in off the coast of Oregon. That evening I saw alto-cumulus clouds moving in. A sure sign the weather was changing.

The next morning I was awakened by the shutters rattling. A strong wind was buffeting the lookout and low dark clouds had moved in. The wind was howling with gusts of 40 or 50 miles-per-hour; so hard it could knock a man off balance. Except for duties that took me outside, I stayed inside. Around 1 p.m. the wind eased, the temperature dropped and it began to rain. Showers at first, but it soon turned to a steady, heavy downpour. It rained all day. Bessie accumulated about an inch of rain.

Around five Butte Falls called: "Bessie, this is Butte Falls."

"This is Bessie, go ahead."

"Can you be packed up and ready to go by noon tomorrow?"

"10-4 Butte Falls, I'll be ready."

"Gordon will be there to help close down the lookout, have a good evening Lloyd."

"Good evening Suzie. Bessie is 10-8.

I relaxed with a cup of coffee and a cigarette and reflected on my summer with Bessie as rain pounded the roof.

I woke early the next morning and noticed silence. No rain was pelting the roof. I rubbed the sleep from my eyes and looked outside. Snow! It was snowing hard and there was 6 inches of the stuff on the catwalk!

I had an early breakfast while watching the snow. Instead of snow coming down it occasionally snowed up! A gust of wind would hit in Red Blanket Canyon and move upslope, blowing the snow with it. The snow would go straight up for 10 or 15 minutes. It was a fun and interesting phenomenon to watch.

After breakfast I began packing up everything I could but there were things I couldn't pack until Gordon arrived. The propane I needed for heat, my refrigerated foods needed to stay cool and I couldn't empty the water cans. If for some reason Gordon failed to arrive I would need those things. I dusted and swept then went through all the cupboards and drawers putting everything in its place so the lookout would be neat for the next fire season. I was done long before noon and spent the rest of my time relaxing and watching the snow. Around noon I saw Gordon and the pack train approaching the foot of the rock. Gordon wore a heavy coat and was squinting in the whirling snow. I went out and told him I would start lowering loads down on the crane. After getting my personal gear on the ground I went in, keyed the mike on the radio and spoke my last message:

"Bessie Rock is ten-seven for the season."

I packed the radio and my refrigerator foods, then emptied the water cans and sent them down to Gordon. I took about an hour to get everything down in the blowing snow and I was getting cold. The snow was about 10 inches deep by this time. I hollered to Gordon, "C'mon up."

Gordon joined me in the cabin and we talked about the summer while drinking the last of my coffee. When we were warm, we turned off the heater, stove and refrigerator; stepped outside and locked the door. We began the task of lowering the shutters. They were heavy with snow and it was a daunting job, but we got them down and secured. The lookout was the way I found it last spring. There was no time for goodbyes, it was snowing hard and the animals were waiting. I was glad for the safety belt on my last trip down the ladder. The rungs were slick with ice and snow.

I helped Gordon load the packs on the pack saddles and he swung to his saddle. I slogged along behind in what was now a foot of snow. At the corner where the rock went out of sight I paused and waved to Bessie and said: "Bye Bessie, see you next year!" And down the hill we went as fast as we could. The snow depth decreased as we lost altitude so when we got to Bessie Shelter it was only about 8 inches. I was glad because my car had no chains and my tires weren't that good.

There were hunters camped in the shelter and we warmed up by their fire. I loaded my gear in the car and helped Gordon load the stock truck. After a couple of weeks of sitting idle I wondered if my car would start. It did! Now the real test. I followed Gordon to the Bessie Rock Road. He had chains on. The last 50 feet was uphill. I paused and waited for Gordon to get far ahead then made a run at it and with a little slipping and sliding I slid onto the Bessie Rock road. From there it was all downhill to the Prospect road. Whew! The snow eased as we went down, and at about 3500 feet elevation it turned to rain.

At the junction with the Prospect road, Gordon stopped and checked the animals. We took his chains off and swung onto the Prospect road. I was headed for Butte Falls and Gordon to Lodgepole. I was wet, but warm and happy to be going to see Linda. Gordon honked at the Lodgepole road as he turned off and I honked back. It was 10 miles to Butte Falls.

AFTERWARDS

The District Ranger greeted me on my return and told me they had a couple more weeks work for me if I wanted it. I did. I didn't know it at the time but he saw potential in me, potential I didn't know I had. I stayed until mid-November and had the opportunity to be with Linda and visit my friends. I relished that last few weeks in Butte Falls. On my last day the Ranger took me to his office and offered me a job for the next year. I wanted it and wanted to return to Bessie. Randy assured me I could.

With money I had saved on Bessie I had bought car parts and tuned up my car. I bought "new" recap tires for the long trip home. On my last day Linda and I vowed to write and I said my goodbyes to the many friends I had made. Early the next morning I took off for California. I had mixed emotions. I was sad to be leaving Butte Falls, but looked forward to seeing my mom and brothers.

I spent the winter on my savings and unemployment checks. As I remember they were about $39 a week in those days. After helping mom with household expenses I had enough that I didn't need to look for work. I spent my time visiting old classmates and waiting for spring when I could return to Butte Falls.

One day I got a letter from Butte Falls asking me if I could go to work at the end of March. I was ecstatic and wrote back immediately. Yes!

When I returned they put me to work with Chuck Hayes marking and cruising timber sales until Bessie was open. But when it came time they wanted me to stay on the timber crew. They had invested money in training me. Randy took me aside one day and said if I stayed with Timber Management he would give me a Forest Technician job. That was a full time job. I wanted to go to Bessie but couldn't resist the prospects of a full time job. I took it. It was hard saying no to Bessie, but I had to think of my future.

The rest is history. My plan to go to Oregon State College never materialized. I spent 35 years with the Forest Service mostly working in Timber Management and doing other jobs as needed. I worked with trail crews, fought fires; a host of odd jobs. I loved lookouts so whenever a lookout needed a break or had to go back to college before the end of fire season I volunteered to take his place. I spent time on every lookout on the District: Rustler Peak, Blue Rock, Devils Peak and Buck Point. Buck Point was an emergency lookout, only staffed during lightning storms and extreme fire conditions. It was an 8-foot by 8-foot cabin with a fire finder in it, and for day-use only. You took a portable radio and enough food for the day with you and returned home late at night. Sadly, I never made it back to Bessie Rock. A few years after I left Bessie the District boundary changed and Bessie ended up on the Prospect District.

Around 1967 the Forest Service went to aerial fire detection. An airplane flew over the District twice a day, and during and after thunderstorms. They began decommissioning lookouts. Usually only one lookout remained on each District. On the Butte Falls District it was, and still is Rustler Peak. Bessie Rock Lookout was decommissioned in 1969. Glass and metal was packed out and the cabin was burned. It was a sad ending to grand old lookout.

After I retired the Forest Service would call and offer me a part-time job whenever they needed a replacement lookout. I spent time on Halls Point, Rustler, and Robinson Butte on the Ashland Ranger District. I spent a lot of time on Robinson; one stretch was over a month. Robinson Butte has a road to it and was about an hour drive from Butte Falls, so I could come down evenings if I chose. But I chose to stay at the lookout most nights.

Then one day I got a call from a lady who had contracted to staff three lookouts on the Umpqua National Forest. She asked me if I would consider spending a summer on Pickett Butte near Tiller Oregon. The pay wasn't much but I had a hard time resisting another summer on a lookout. I insisted that I needed 2 days off to tend to household chores and my garden. Pickett Butte was about a 2-hour drive, so I could return home evenings if I was needed. I agreed to do it and spent that summer there. It was much different than my time on Bessie, but that's another story.

Bessie Rock Today.
The lookout sat on the far rock with the large boulder on it.

An Osborne Fire Finder like I used on Bessie.

Bessie Shelter Today—In 1957 it was the
trailhead for the Bessie Rock Trail

AFTERTHOUGHTS

I have had many adventures with the time I spent in the
woods with the Forest Service and the time backpacking into the
wilderness for recreation. At one time or another I took all six of
my children backpacking and camping in the Sky Lakes Wilderness
Area at Blue Canyon. In 1993 I hiked from Lake of the Woods to
the Columbia River on the Pacific Crest Trail, a distance of 430
miles. My only companion was my dog Le Pooch. I have made many
friends on my adventures and have beautiful memories.

While Bessie was not my first job with the Forest Service, it
was my first job where I was responsible for the outcome. I was
responsible for the locating and reporting fires, for the care of the
lookout, and for giving a good impression to visitors. I learned much
on Bessie such as how to make-do when resources were sparse or

lacking and how to cope with being alone for long stretches. At the very top of that list of beautiful memories is the summer I spent with my friend Bessie.

Bessie Rock has a road to it now. Occasionally on a warm summer day I drive up to the rock with a cold beer and drink a toast to Bessie and Me.

"Thirty-Four Degrees Year 'Round"

"Scoop up the water and the moon is in your hands;
Hold the flowers and your clothes are scented with them."
(Zen Saying)

INTRODUCTION

I was 20 years old and it was my second year (1958) working for the Butte Falls Ranger District. I worked for the Timber Management Department, but it wasn't a full time job so occasionally I did other work. I planted and pruned trees, did campground and trail maintenance work. The story I relate here is about one of those days on trail maintenance.

THE CREW

Our foreman for the day was Corbet Smith. Corbet was an old-timer around Butte Falls. He's been a logger for Owen-Oregon Lumber Company when the railroad ran up from Medford. He was a timber-faller before chainsaws came into common use, and trees were fell with back-breaking crosscuts. Corbet was a big, strong, man with a steady hand and a clear head. He spent much of his time hunting and fishing and knew the local area well. He was nearing 70 years old and retirement. I respected him. He was a good choice for foreman of our small trail crew.

The second member of the crew was Charlie. Charlie is in his 40's and spent most of his life around Butte Falls working at various jobs. He was from a big family and his parents, siblings, uncles, aunts and cousins are scattered around the Upper Rogue Country. They make up a large portion of Butte Fall's population. Charlie, his wife and their covey of kids lived below Butte Falls a few miles. Charlie was a rounder and a heavy drinker with a habit of showing up for work late, or not at all. That habit, plus the fact that he was uneducated and couldn't read or write, accounts for the fact that he had trouble keeping a steady job.

A few years before I arrived in Butte Falls Charlie landed a job on the Butte Falls Ranger District. Fire Control Officer Doug Finch took Charlie under his wing and overlooked some of his shortcomings. Charlie was appreciative and did Doug a good job. When Charlie did show up for work he was a hard worker, knew his job and the country well and was a decent companion.

I made up the final and least experienced member of the crew. I had enough experience to know what the job was and how to accomplish it but didn't know the country. This would be my first trip into Blue Canyon.

THE TASK

Our task was to maintain the Blue Canyon Trail from its trailhead near Blue Rock Lookout to Island Lake, a distance of about 5.5 miles. In 1958 this area was designated as a Primitive Area, now it's part of the Sky Lakes Wilderness; all pristine mountains, lakes, meadows, and forest. I was looking forward to the hike. It's the high-mountain country that I love.

Trial maintenance consist of cutting fallen trees out of the trail, cleaning and reconstructing water bars; and removing boulders and limbs from the trail tread.

We arrived at the trail-head at about 9 a.m. and gather our gear from the bed of the pickup. Corbet leads the way carrying a shovel in one hand and Pulaski in the other. Charlie follows carrying the chainsaw pack which included the saw, fuel, chain oil and wedges. It's a pretty heavy load. I follow Charlie carrying a pack with our lunches, and some chainsaw tools in it. I carry a hoe in one hand. We have no canteen since water was readily available along the trail.

For the first mile the trail goes down at a pretty steep grade and the rule is the steeper the trail the more water-bars. Most that we come across had taken a pretty good beating during last fall's rains and the spring snowmelt, so we spend a lot of time repairing the drainage system. It was a clear, warm day and hot, dusty work. I sweat enough and breathe in enough dust that by the time we come to Round Lake about a mile down the trail I've worked up a mighty big thirst.

We stop, sit down by the trail and take our first break at a spot overlooking the lake. The lake is a glistening blue jewel about 300 feet south of the trail. After having a smoke and resting I suggest we go down to the lake to get a drink.

"Nope!" Charlie says, "Good water up ahead, 34 degrees year 'round."

About that time Corbet stands up and says, "Bout time we move on." and begins walking down the trail.

That was when I begin getting irritated at Charlie. I know him well and am pretty damn sure he'd never carried a thermometer in there and measured the temperature of any water, let alone year 'round! I doubt if he could even read a thermometer. I follow them down the trail and my growing thirst deepens as I watch the glistening, blue waters of Round Lake fade in the distance.

A mile further we come to Blue Lake. It's a stunningly beautiful lake with deep blue waters backed by high cliffs. The trail circles the northern edge of the lake just a few feet from the shoreline. As we near the eastern edge I can see a small stream pouring out of the lake. I am sure that Corbet and Charlie will drop their tools and take a drink of the beautiful clear, gurgling water. But no! They wade across the stream and start up a hill on the trail that now leads away from the lake.

When I get to the stream I stop and yell to them, "Wait up a minute, I am going to get a drink."

"No! That's warm water." Charlie said, "Good water up ahead, 34 degrees year 'round."

Then Corbet, with some authority in his voice said, "Won't be long now. Just around the next bend. Come on Lloyd"

I bite my tongue, grit my teeth, cuss Charlie and his damn "34 degrees," and follow them up the hill; swallowing their dust! My irritation is turning to anger! I'm thirsty damn it! We're passing up beautiful water and the more we pass the greater my thirst becomes! I'm in a surly mood as I follow along.

THE WATER

Then we come to the meadow that surrounds Meadow Lake. My companions leave the trail and go down the hill about 20 feet into the meadow. A stream of water pours out of a pipe that's been driven into the hillside. Hanging on a stem nearby is a cup made from a tin can. Charlie parts the grass and fills the cup. With a broad smile he hands it to me.

I take a sip—It's the nectar of the Gods! Sweet, ice cold, nectar of the Gods!—I drink the entire can of water. I have never tasted water so good! Anything so good! My anger evaporates and I am at peace. I now understand the wisdom of the phrase, "Nope, good water up ahead, 34 degrees year 'round."

I fill the can and pass it to Corbet; he passes it to Charlie. We continue passing the can around until we've had our fill. We sit quietly smoking, letting the awesome silence of the wilderness permeate us. The secret power of the water overtakes us.

Relaxing around the spring we eat our lunch and talk and laugh. We gather up our gear and moved on down the trail to Island Lake, the end of our project. On the way back we again stop at the spring at Meadow Lake for another drink of that pure cold water.

I have never forgotten that day and the magic achieved by the simple act of drinking the water at Meadow Lake.

A few years after that day both Corbet and Charlie have died. Corbet from age related disease and Charlie in an automobile accident. They remain in my memory as part of a special moment in my life.

MANY YEARS LATER

One day many years later, I planned a 3-day trip into Blue Canyon with my oldest daughter Natona, and my youngest son Kevin. I had been in Blue Canyon many times by then. Natona is about 12 or 13 and Kevin is about 6 years old at this time. Natona and I carry the packs with our gear. We plan to camp at Meadow Lake.

We took a break when we reached Round Lake at the same place where Corbet, Charlie and I had rested. As we enjoy the beauty of the lake in the distance one of the kids asked, "I'm thirsty; can we get a drink Dad?"

I couldn't resist. With a silent nod to Charlie I said, "Nope! "Good water up ahead, 34 degrees year 'round."

And we moved on . . . .

Misfire

When I was about 31 years old in the spring of 1970, my boss asked me if I wanted to go to Blasting School.

Blasting school was a one-week training where you learned how to handle various types of dynamite and plastic explosives safely, and how to set up, load, and fire charges. What young man doesn't like to blow things up? Of course I said yes! I learned how to set charges to be exploded electrically with a plunger, and those with blasting caps lit with a match. There were lots of demonstrations blowing up rocks and stumps. It was a fun week and in the end I passed the test and walked away with a Blasting Card which made me a Forest Service Certified Blaster.

That summer I was recruited by fire Control Office Lou Cernick to head up a trail crew to reconstruct up to standards about a half-mile of the Pacific Crest Trail where it goes up to the top of Devils Peak. The elevation of the trail here is above 7500 feet and mostly near or above timberline on a ridge top that is strewn with boulders. Reconstruction will require a lot of blasting.

The crew consisted of Jim Moore, a tall, lanky fellow a little older than me. Jim has a jovial personality full of jokes, and pranks. He's a local that has lived around Butte Falls all of his life. I know him well. He is a hard worker and a great companion. The other member of our gang is a college forestry student about 20 years old. Harold is a quiet, studious type who is also a good worker and companion. Our supervisor, Lou Cernick, is a super guy and a lot of fun to be around. He will, for the most part, be at the Butte Falls Ranger Station in radio contact with us. He will go with us the first day to show us the job and explain what he wants done, and on our last day when he will inspect our job. I have been chosen as foreman since I was the only certified blaster.

It's a 5.5 mile hike in and we will be camped near Heather Ponds. We will work 10 days on with 4 days off. Our camp gear was packed in by Gordon Walker on mules and he and Lou set it all up before we got there. It was a comfortable camp that had a large army tent with sleeping bags and cots. There was a two burner Coleman white gas cook stove, a couple of Coleman lamps and all of the pots, pans and silverware we would need. Gordon also packed in all of the plastic powder, dynamite and caps along with our tools.

Jim, Harold and I figured out what food we wanted and went to Medford to buy it. I was a cigarette smoker in those days, but because I couldn't smoke when working around dynamite I got me a couple of cans of Copenhagen snuff. I'd chewed the stuff before and it took away the craving for nicotine.

On our first day we met Gordon and Lou at the Seven Lakes Basin trailhead and Gordon packed all of our personal gear and food on mules. We took off walking up the trail while Gordon followed us riding horseback and leading the pack train. In about 4 miles we came to the Devils Peak Trail Junction and took it. The pleasant aroma of the hemlock-Shasta fir forest, the pure mountain breeze and the awesome alpine scenery all combined to make it a pleasant and rewarding hike. The high mountain country is something I have always loved. About 1.5 miles up the Devils Peak Trail we intersected the Pacific Crest Trail, and very near that was our camp at Heather Ponds.

After storing our gear in the tent Lou led us up the trail about a quarter-mile to where our job started. He told us our job was to widen the trail-way to at least 8 feet wide and smooth out the trail bed up to the Summit of Devils Peak, a distance of roughly a half-mile. Gordon pointed out several spots where it is difficult to get mules loaded with packs through. I could see it would be slow going. It takes time to carefully set charges then clear the debris caused by the blast, but I was anxious to begin in the morning.

Back at camp we said goodbye to Lou and Gordon and they headed down the trail to home. We arranged our gear and stored our food. We were cautious about food because animals have good noses and we sure didn't want a bear coming in our tent in the middle of the night looking for a tasty morsel. Black bears are common in this area and more than one surprised back-country camp has been raided.

We found a place where digging in the gravel and sand was relatively easy and after carefully wrapping our meat we buried it about 18 inches deep. We hoped to keep it cool and hopefully block its scent from animals.

We rounded up a big pile of firewood and built a fire about 10 feet from opening of the tent. We hoped to keep the fire going all night as a warning to bears. Then we brewed up a pot of camp coffee and sat around the fire taking stock of what we had done, making sure we hadn't missed anything. Our water would come out of one of the Heather Ponds. These are small shallow ponds and they heat up quickly in the sun. Its tepid water with a lot of algae and bugs, so to purify it we strained out the bugs and boiled the water. After boiling it we let it sit out overnight to cool off to make passable drinking water. We used the other Heather Pond for bathing.

I'm a pretty good cook, and so is Jim so all of our meals were pretty darn tasty. As I recall we had grilled steaks, baked potato and canned veggies for dinner that first evening. After cleaning up we sat around the fire and had a smoke while telling tall tales. Neither Jim nor I had worked with Harold before so we spent time getting acquainted with our companion.

Jim is an avid card player and we had brought a deck. About dusk we set up a box in the tent to use as a table; arranged a couple of the cots for seating, and a Coleman lamp for light, then began playing cards. That was the beginning of a fierce competition between Jim and I that would flourish through our entire stay. We played Pinochle, Casino, Poker and a few other games and kept a running total of the winner of each game. We didn't need to worry about a bear raiding camp while we played because we were loud and raucous as we waved our arms and yelled at the cards and each other.

Eating dinner, relaxing around the fire, then playing cards became the ritual we practiced our entire stay. It was a lot of fun.

In spite of living in the country all of his life, Jim had developed one of those irrational fears as a child that had stuck with him into adulthood. He was afraid of the dark. When we crawled in our sleeping bags he wasn't too happy when we turned off the lamp, so he kept a flashlight nearby. The fire outside the tent provided a little light that flowed through the tent walls and was some comfort. Whenever he woke up in the night Jim would go out and stoke up the fire then put some more wood on. We had no trouble keeping our fire going all night.

Up early the next day we ate bacon, eggs and fried taters. After washing dishes we grabbed our tools and headed to our powder stash where we loaded what we needed in packs. Harold and I carried packs with plastic powder while Jim had a pack with snacks, blasting caps, and a gallon canteen of drinking water. It was taboo to carry powder and blasting caps in the same pack for obvious reasons. We also had an electric generator attached to a handle that when twisted created an electric charge, and about 250 feet of heavy duty insulated wire that ran from the plunger to the blast site.

A little about the powder we were using. Dynamite comes in sticks, usually colored red. It's the stuff you see the coyote using in the Road Runner cartoons. It's great for blasting stumps and holes, and even rocks if you have a rock drill to provide a hole for it. But we had no drill. One disadvantage is that in older sticks the nitroglycerin begins to leak into the waxed paper that covers it, and most people develop headaches while handling the stuff. I'm one of those people.

Plastic powder comes in a block. It has the consistency of a child's modeling clay and a portion of the block can be cut off and molded to rocks or packed in crevasses. It is perfect for the job we were doing. Handling it doesn't cause headaches in most people.

At the beginning of our work we surveyed the area and marked rocks that needed to be blasted. Some were the tops of boulders protruding through the pathway. Others were rocks protruding in from the sides of the trail in places that needed widening. We usually set 5 to 10 charges at each setting.

After determining what places needed shot we began setting the charges using the plastic powder. Once done molding the powder to the rocks I sent Jim down the trail about 400 feet and Harold up the trail. They acted as lookouts to alert any trail travelers that blasting was about to take place. Meanwhile, I took an electrical cap and inserted it into the plastic powder at each shot, then I cut off a length of two-strand wire from a spool, hooked a red-plus wire and a minus-white wire to the cap, then ran the wire over to our long main wire that ran up the trail 250 feet. With each shot all set, I wired them all to the mainline and we were ready to shoot. I always kept the plunger with me so no one could accidentally plunge it and blow me to smithereens while I was working alone.

I walked up the trail to the other end of our main wire where Harold was and wired the main line to the plunger. Everything was in place now. As loud as I could I yelled a warning, "FIRE!" When Jim heard my yell he looked up and down the trial to make sure no one was on it. If not, he yelled back, "FIRE!" After hearing Jim I paused a few minutes and repeated, "FIRE!" Jim responded, "FIRE!" We did that one more time. Three times in all and on Jim's last "FIRE!" I twisted the handle.

BOOM! And a few small rocks came clattering around us from the blast. The explosion echoed off the surrounding mountains and a cloud of dust began to rise. I lit a cigarette and took a break. It was always a relief when our shot had worked.

I walked alone back into the blast zone and inspected everything to make sure all of the charges had exploded. When I was sure I yelled, "ALL CLEAR!" Jim and Harold rejoined me and we would begin the task of clearing out the debris. About 25% of the time our shots didn't get the results we had hoped for so we would have to re-shoot those areas.

On that first day while were clearing debris we heard someone else blasting in our area. We found out that another crew was working on the Seven Lakes Basin trail near Middle Lake. They were about an air-mile away from us, but about 1500 feet in elevation below us down in the forest. They were shooting mostly stumps and their shots came through to us loud and clear. They were camped at Grass Lake and we were a little jealous because Grass Lake was a very good fishing hole.

We could usually set, blast and clear out about 6 to 10 shots a day. That first day went well and we all learned our jobs so from then on we worked like a well-oiled machine. It was a good crew and we worked well together.

We usually got to work around six or seven in the morning and got back to camp at three or four. One day we got done early, so Harold and I decided to visit the other crew at Grass Lake. We hiked cross country straight down the steep mountainside below camp until we caught the Seven Lakes Trail, then hiked north on the trail to Grass Lake. It took less than a half-hour to arrive at their camp. They were glad to see us and compare notes on our jobs. We spent a pleasant hour drinking coffee and chatting with the guys and they gave us some fresh trout for dinner. Then we headed back to our camp.

About the fourth day into our stay we had just completed putting the plastic powder in place for about seven shots. Harold and Jim stayed with me while I began putting caps in them and wired it all up. Harold wanted to learn the procedure. Jim got a bit antsy about just sitting around and watching so he grabbed a hoe and went up the trail a ways to do some clearing on the path. When I got done I yelled to him we that we were ready to fire. He came ambling back with his long, lanky legs, but he had forgot there were wires crossing the trail and he walked into them and got couple tangled around his feet, pulling the caps out of the powder as he walked. Both Harold and I yelled "Jim Stop!" He did, and realized what he had done. He stood still as we grabbed the caps and unwrapped the wires. That spooked us all because while the caps are made to discharge with an electrical charge, they can go off if struck with a hard enough force. The caps that had pulled out had bounced off rocks.

The guys went to their position up and down the trail and I reset the caps and checked the rest of the charges. The blast went off as planned, but we all learned to keep aware of the wires on the trail!

Late into our stay we had about 10 charges all set to go off. Jim and Harold were in their positions and I checked everything before walking up the trail to the plunger. After going through the ritual of yelling a warning "FIRE' three times I twisted the plunger and there was silence! Nothing but birds tweeting. It was the dreaded misfire. I contemplated on what to do for a while then yelled down to Jim, "Stay put, we've had a misfire."

I know what the book says. I learned it in Blasting School. You are supposed to stay out of the blast area, and make sure no one enters it for 24 hours. That meant that we would all have to stay at our post until dark, then Harold and I would have to make a wide detour around the blast zone in order to get back to camp. I also know that rule was made for fire fuses. Sometimes after the fuse was lit it would smolder and burn slow so you had no idea when it might reach the charge and go off. That's why the 24-hour rule. The rule stayed in place even though electric fuses were now commonly used.

I made a decision and hollered to Jim, "We're going to stay put for two hour then I'm going back to reset everything." He answered "OK."

Harold and I got comfortable and chatted while the 2 hours elapsed. Finally I grabbed the plunger and began walking cautiously down to the blast zone. I mean to tell you that even though I calculated that it was safe, it was mega spooky walking down there. I made it to the blast area and inspected everything. I couldn't see anything wrong. I figured that somewhere we had a bad connection in the wiring so I replaced all the wires that ran from the caps to the main wire. I twisted all the plus wires together then did the same to the minus wires. I was now ready to attach those twisted wires to the main wire that ran up the hill. After a half hour working in a misfired blast zone my nerves were on edge. I picked up the main wire and attached the plus wires to the plus lead. One more group of wires to attach and I would be done and could get out of there. Very carefully I brought the minus wires to the minus lead and just as I began to attach it I heard a loud BOOM!

I about crapped my pants! It took me a few seconds to realize the BOOM was from the other crew working down by Middle Lake. But with my nerves already on edge I needed to sit down and calm down. To hell with the rules, I sat, lit a cigarette and thanked God!

It took about 15 minutes to calm my nerves enough to go back and attach the minus wires. Then I grabbed the plunger and headed up the hill, glad to be out of there. Back on top I attached the plunger to the main wire and went through the ritual of yelling "FIRE!" three times then twisted the plunger and we heard a loud BOOM! The misfire was no longer a misfire.

Back at camp I explained to Jim and Harold why it took me so long and what happened as I was attaching the last wire. It was great to be alive to tell them.

The morning before we were to pack up camp Lou showed up. He arrived about 10 AM while we were setting off our last shots and doing some smoothing of the path. He joined us and we finished the job around noon.

We had used up nearly all of the plastic powder but we still had six cases of dynamite. Lou had brought it here to dispose of it if we didn't use it up. It had been stored for a long time and was leaking nitro-glycerin, making it unstable.

Lou likes to blow things up too, so to dispose of the dynamite he decided to make one big boom and set off all six cases at once. We found a flat spot on top of the ridge we were on, opened one of the cases and placed a cap in a stick of dynamite. We replaced the stick in the box and closed it with our lead wire running out. Then we stacked the remaining boxes on top of it. Lou ran the wire to our main wire and hooked it up. He sent Jim down and me up the Seven Lakes trail to act as lookout. Harold went down the Pacific Trail. Lou strung out the main wire to some large boulders 250 feet away that would give him some protection if anything flew his way since 250 feet is not a long way when setting off six cases of dynamite.

When he was all set he hollered "FIRE;" we all answered "FIRE." We did it two more times and Lou twisted the handle. Not just a BOOM but a KER-BOOM! A very loud, powerful explosion shot into the air followed by an immense dust cloud. The sound of the blast echoed off the surrounding mountains for what seemed like forever, sounding like rolling thunder. We loved it and began hollering, "Yahoo." Boys will be boys!

All of the dynamite was destroyed and very little damage was done to the rocks around the blast. Most of the force of the shot went up in the air.

We gathered up all of our tools and went to camp where we said goodbye to Lou who was going home. We would spend our last night there and take down camp the next morning. Gordon would meet us with his mules to pack our gear out.

After dinner that night we went in the tent to play our last rounds of cards. Jim and I had got into a dispute about who had won the most games of Casino so far. We had lost track and each thought he was ahead. After some friendly bantering and defending our positions we decided that the last game we played would be Casino, and the winner of that would be champion card player of Devils Peak. And we agreed that no matter who won, in the morning we would tear up those damn cards and burn them. Jim won!

Up early the next morning we had a hearty breakfast, finishing it off with hot chocolate and coffee. Then true to our word we each took a portion of the deck of cards, tore them up and threw them in the fire. We were in high spirits and laughing all the time and of course Jim couldn't help reminding me that he was the champion card player of Devils Peak.

We were done tearing the camp down and rolling and packing it all up in about two hours and shortly after Gordon showed up with the mules. We helped him load the pack string and then headed down the trail to home. I had mixed emotions. I would miss our camp up in alpine country with good friends, but then I had a family I missed at home.

When I started writing this story I gave a call to Jim to see if his memory of the events were the same as mine and see what he might add. As soon as I reminded him of our trip he yelled, "I won! I'm the champion card player!" After all these years he couldn't resist reminding me that he had won. Then he laughed, "Remember tearing up those damn cards and burning them?" Yes, it was a good trip full of fun memories!

The Perfect Day

It's seldom in one's life that we have one of those days where everything goes right and we can do a fist pump and say, "Yes! I nailed it!" One day on Buck Point I had one of those days.

It was a warm sunny morning in Butte Falls when the Butte Falls Ranger District Fire Control Officer ask me if I wanted to go to Buck Point as lookout for the day. The southern Oregon area had a 90% chance of afternoon and evening thunderstorms. I was more than happy to get out of my Timber Management routine and spend the day watching lightning from Buck Point and readily agreed.

Buck Point is about 20 miles from Butte Falls and knowing I could be there until midnight I went home and made a large lunch I could snack on all day. At the Ranger Station I grabbed a large topographic map of the area, some lookout tools, and a portable radio. I always carried a compass. When I was fully prepared I grabbed a Forest Service pickup and headed towards the Point. The pickup also had a Forest Service radio so I had backup.

Buck Point once was an emergency lookout with an 8-foot by 8-foot cabin with an Osborne Fire Finder in it, but that had been torn down long ago when the Rogue River National Forest went to aerial fire detection. Contracted airplanes fly a Forest Service spotter around the district at intervals, and during and after thunderstorms. Only one lookout, Rustler Peak, remained on the District. The District often sends someone to Buck Point when the fire danger is high because a stationary lookout sometimes has the advantage over spotter plane.

I arrived at the end of the Buck Point road at about 9 a.m. From there it is about a 100-foot hike up a steep rocky trail to the summit of the peak. I grabbed my gear and a few snacks and hiked up.

The Point is a rocky promontory right at 5000 feet elevation with cliffs on three sides and a steep sloping grade down the south side where the pickup was parked. It has a great view to the north. Nearly the entire south end of the Butte Falls District is visible including all of the western slopes of Mt McLoughlin. Bieberstedt Butte is to the south and a little higher than Buck Point. It blocks much of the views in that direction, however views to the southeast are pretty good.

I settled in, poured some coffee, lit a smoke and watched as cumulus clouds began building up over the surrounding mountains. Sometime around 1 p.m. the bases of the clouds began to darken and I began to hear the rumbles of thunder echoing off the hills. A short time later a dark cloud covered the sky over Buck Point and it began to hail. Just a few large hailstones at first but it soon increased to a pounding hail storm with lightning and thunder. I was unprotected and decided prudence was the better part of valor. I retreated to the pickup where I was protected from lightning and out of the hail and rain.

The storm was moving northeast and when I turned on the pickup's Forest Service radio I could hear other lookouts and observers reporting smokes south and west of me on the Ashland and Applegate Districts. Robinson Butte lookout on the Ashland District was not far from me; about 5.5 miles to my southeast. I heard no activity from him so I assumed he was still in the midst of storms as I was. The storm lasted about 45 minutes and when I felt it was safe I returned to my post on top of the Point. It was still sprinkling lightly.

I got out my binoculars and started scanning the county around me. Fog pockets were rising out of the canyons everywhere making it difficult to spot any smoke. I began scanning the higher ridges and soon I spotted a small column of smoke on the western flanks of Mt. McLoughlin. I took an azimuth as best as I could with my hand compass then spread out my map. The fire was about a quarter-mile northeast of South Squaw Tip, a volcanic cinder cone on the flanks of the mountain. I marked an x on the map where I estimated it was and wrote down a legal description then got on the radio.

"Butte Falls this is Buck Point with a fire report."

"This is Butte Falls, go ahead Lloyd." I recognized Jacks voice.

"Azimuth 86 degrees, distance to fire 7 miles, Legal Description is northeast of the northeast quarter, Section 15, Township 36 south, Range 4 east. The fire is about a quarter-mile slightly northeast of South Squaw Tip on the flanks of Mt. McLoughlin. There is a small column of smoke coming from a forested area just below timberline. I estimate the size as 1/10 acre or less.

"Ten-four Lloyd. Is there much wind on the mountain?"

"No not too much the column is mostly rising straight up."

"Ten-four"

Immediately Jack called Rustler Peak, "Rustler did you hear the report Buck Point gave?"

"Yes", the fellow said. "I have an azimuth for that fire," and he proceeded to give Butte Falls his azimuth.

"And I put the fire in the same location Buck Point has it."

"Thanks Rustler, We'll get a crew moving on that fire. Butte Falls."

I spent the next hour scanning the country with binoculars. The fog pockets were dissipating and I could see in to the canyons and hollows better, but I saw no other smokes. I sat down and grabbed a snack and out of the corner of my eye I saw a small white puff rising out of the canyon of the North Fork of Little Butte Creek to my southeast. It was at the base of Robinson Butte very near the creek. I quickly stood up and put the binoculars on the area. By that time the puff had mostly disappeared. I marked the spot in my mind. Was it smoke? It looked like it. But it could have been a fog pocket. I wasn't sure. I continued scanning the country around me paying particular attention to where I had saw the mysterious puff. About 20 minutes passed and then another puff appeared. I got a good look at it before it disappeared and this time I was sure. It was smoke! It wasn't much smoke, just a small puff that quickly disappeared in the breeze. I marked in my mind a large tree near where the puff appeared for use getting my azimuth then went to work getting the azimuth and legal description. State Highway 140 ran just north of the North Fork of Little Butte Creek and the fire was just south of the creek, putting it on the Ashland Ranger District. I called Ashland, "Ashland, this is Buck Point with a fire report."

"This is Ashland, go ahead Buck Point."

"Azimuth from Buck Point is 150 degrees. Distance to fire is 5.1 miles. Legal is southeast of the northeast, section 5, Township 37 south, Range 4 east. Fire is putting up intermittent puffs of smoke. I estimate size as less than 1/10 acre. Slight breeze blowing in the area."

"Ten four Buck Point. Air-One did you hear that?"

"Yes, we are on the south end of your District now. Will be there in that area in about 10 minutes and will give it a look."

Air-One is the spotter plane that was in the air searching for fires on the Ashland, Butte Falls and Prospect Districts since shortly after the storms went through. The spotter plane has a distinct advantage over a stationary lookout since he can circle a location and view it from different angles and heights. His disadvantage is that he usually stays over a given area only a short time.

Soon I could hear Air-One approaching and saw him when he got north of Robinson Butte. He circled my fire about three times giving it a good look then, "Ashland this is Air-One."

"This is Ashland."

"We gave that area around North Fork Little Butte Creek a good look and we are seeing nothing."

"Ten-four, this is Ashland. Buck Point did you hear that?

"Ten-four, Buck Point."

Air-One had circled the area three times and flew up North Fork Canyon from west to east at a low altitude and saw nothing. The fire had not flared up with a puff of smoke, or it had went out which is not unusual when fires start under heavy thunderstorm showers like we had.

I continued my search, but still paid particular attention to the area around the North Fork.

Puff! There it was again. Another puff of smoke rose out of the canyon and quickly disappeared in the breeze. "Ashland this is Buck Point."

"Go ahead Buck Point."

"That fire near the North Fork is still putting up intermittent smokes."

"Ten-four Buck Point. Air-One are you in that area?"

"This is Air-One, we are near Rustler Peak. We'll go back and take another look."

"Ten-four, Ashland."

I could see Air-One as he flew south from Rustler Peak. Soon he was circling my fire again. He circled it four or five times and flew the canyon up and down. He spent more time than he had on his first trip, but no puffs of smoke appeared during his search. Finally, "Ashland this is Air-One."

"Go ahead Air-one."

I heard a clearly irritated spotter explain, "There is no fire there. There are still a few fog pockets rising out of the canyon. Buck Point is seeing fog."

"Ten-four Air-One, this is Ashland."

Now if you want to get an experienced lookout mad that's the way to do it! Broadcast all over the National Forest for all to hear that he is reporting fog as a fire! I was fit to be tied! I had worked on the Ashland District and the folks knew me. They weren't ready to buy the line that I was reporting fog. I heard, "Buck Point this is Ashland."

"This is Buck Point."

"Keep an eye on that area. We have a standby crew nearby and we are sending them down Highway 140 to a place across the canyon and see if they can spot it from that vantage point. Your contact with the crew is Joe."

"Ten-four Ashland, this is Buck Point."

About 10 minutes elapsed when I heard Joe call Ashland, "We are parked off 140 and have a good view of the reported location of the fire."

"Ten-four Joe, just hang out there until further notice

After a long wait, there it was again! Puff! Another puff of smoke rose out of the canyon. I didn't report it. I waited to see if the standby crew saw it. They had, "Ashland this is Joe."

"Go ahead Joe."

"We see the fire. Its right where Buck Point put it. It is in the dead top of a large Douglas-fir. We'll need an experienced timber faller to get it down. We see from our map that we can get a better, shorter route to the fire if we go around, cross the creek and get on Forest Road 3702. When we get there we will send traveling instructions for the faller."

"Ten-four Joe. Notify us when you get to the fire. Ashland."

Bingo! Yes! I nailed it! I'd out-spotted Air-One and I knew that he and all of the Rogue River National Forest could hear our conversations. So much for fog!

There was no more activity the rest of the day and Jack released me around 11 p.m. As I drove to Butte Falls in the dark I was feeling good. I spotted and got the location of two fires right on the money and I had out spotted an irritating air spotter. It had been the perfect day!

A Mountain Of Many Names

I t only seems fitting that I should end this book with a story about "The Mountain of Many Names," Mt. McLaughlin, or as I prefer to call it Mt. Pit. The story is about the mountain, me and my dog Le Pooch (Pooch for short). I was 53 when I retired from the Forest Service and still in good shape. A dream of mine was to hike the Pacific Crest Trail (PCT). It wasn't possible for me to hike the entire trail from Mexico to Canada, so I settled on hiking the trail though most of Oregon. I began my journey at Fourmile Lake in Southern Oregon and hiked to the Columbia River a distance of 430 miles. Pooch was my companion. We completed our trip in early September of 1994 and to keep fit I decided to climb the Mt. Pit from the east side and spend a night on top.

Pooch was about two years old when I acquired him for the expressed purpose of hiking with me and being my watchdog around our camps. His history was that he had been a stray hanging around the few scattered homes about three miles east of Butte Falls for nearly a year. He lived off the land and whatever he could beg from the surrounding community. I'd heard about him and he sounded like the right age and size dog for my needs. I told a friend, Jan Werren, about my need for a dog. She lived in the area where he hung around and captured him for me. Diane and I went up and took him for a ride and hike. Pooch had not shed his stray ways and as soon as he was out of our sight he ran wild through the woods. We didn't find him until the next morning. It was a shaky start, but we decided to adopt him.

I have owned dogs nearly my entire life but no dog became as close to me as Pooch. During our hike we hiked together, ate together, overcame obstacles together and slept together 24 hours a day, 7 days a week for 43 days and nights. We bonded! Before it was over we knew each other's habits and feelings, and anticipated each other's next move. Pooch made it clear that he knew how to survive on his own and didn't need a master. We would instead be companions. Though he has now died he remains to this day as my best friend.

I will relate one event that happened on our PCT hike to give you an idea of Pooch's instincts. We were hiking down a long hill though forested terrain as we descended into the Columbia River Gorge. From studying the map I knew we would be coming to a creek shortly. No problem, I had crossed hundreds of creeks on our journey.

It was Pooch's habit to run 300 to 500 yards down the trail ahead of me and then return to make sure I was still coming. He would then whirl around and do the same thing over. As we neared the creek Pooch came running back, but this time he didn't whirl around, instead he got beside me and walked close. So close I almost tripped over him. He was wet, so I knew that he had been to the creek. When we came to the creek, I saw it was a slow moving stream a few inches deep and 12 feet wide. No problem. Before crossing I sat down and took a break. Pooch sat with me. Strange behavior for a dog that liked to be far out in front.

After my break I rose and began putting my pack on. Pooch went across the creek and sat on the other side watching me. I approached the stream and began wading across and Whoa! I lost my balance! The moss on the bottom of the stream was as slick as a bar of wet soap. Fortunately I had a walking stick and was able to regain my balance. I continued across cautiously and when I reached the other bank Pooch whirled and down the trail he went, resuming his old habits.

As time passed I came to believe that Pooch was aware that a two footed man with boots was at risk crossing that slick stream. Nothing like a four-pawed dog with claws. He wanted to make sure he was there to help. That is the only thing that explains his strange behavior of staying with me until I had safely crossed the stream, and it illustrates the incredible instincts and concern for me that Pooch had gained.

I had climbed Mt. Pit in the early "60's" with co-worker and friend, Al McCorkandale. We had climbed the northwest ridge, a tougher climb than my planned route up the east side. The east side is a 5.5 mile hike with the first 4.5 miles being an uphill walk on a trail through forest. The last mile is above timberline on a steep rocky ridge with no trail. The normal route is to just stay on top of the ridge to the summit. While not a technical climb it still is a hard climb up the steep boulder strewn ridge.

I planned to camp on the summit so I was carrying a pack which made the climb tougher. Normally my hiking pack weighed 55 pounds. For this climb I had pared it down to 40 pounds. Pooch carried a doggie pack that I normally filled to 15 pounds, but for this trip it was 10 pounds. The main creator of weight was water. Except for a quart canteen I usually didn't carry water while back-packing. I got my water from springs and lakes, but with the exception of snowdrifts near the top, there was no water source on the mountain. I put a gallon in Le Pooch's pack and I carried a gallon in mine. That along with my quart canteen should be enough.

It was about 8:00 AM when we arrived at the trailhead. I had brought a cooler filled with a six-pack of beer and ice that I stowed in the front seat then locked the pickup. Then I let Pooch out of the bed and grabbed his pack. There is nothing in the world that Pooch loves better than to be hiking in the woods with me and when he sees his pack he knows we will soon be on our way. He always he gets excited, twirling in circles and rolling on his back. I had been through this many times and it was always a difficult chore getting the loaded pack strapped on a very excited dog. After doing a double check to make sure I had everything I hefted my pack on. Pooch and I were on our way to our next adventure.

In the cool mountain air the hike through the forest was refreshing and true to form Pooch was far out in front of me, returning periodically to make sure I was still coming. Somewhere along the way I noticed a slight but persistent pain in my right knee. I had my hiking pole with me and could relieve the pain by taking a little weight off with the pole. I wasn't concerned.

In about an hour and a half we reached a rocky ridge at timberline. From here on we would be walking up the ridge, I stopped and Pooch and I shared a snack and some water before starting the steep climb to the summit. It was slow climbing the ridge as I picked my way around and over boulders. I was extra careful. One misstep and a broken ankle could be life threatening for a lone climber. Pooch, sensing danger, stayed close ahead of me, usually not traveling more than 100 feet up the ridge. I kept my head down as I jumped from boulder to boulder or weaved a path around them. Somehow we got on a minor spur that instead of going up the ridge went around the south side of the mountain. We went about 400 feet on the wrong path before I realized my error. The pain in my knee had increased and I was using my walking stick as a cane more and more. I took a break and contemplated what to do.

I could see the top of the ridge where I was supposed to be about 250 feet nearly straight up the mountainside. Should I backtrack and find the correct route, or should I make the climb up the side of the mountain to the top of the ridge? I was now away from the rocks and boulders and the route straight up was over loose cinders and sand. I decided that backtracking would take longer so in the interest of time I chose to climb straight up.

As I climbed through the loose cinders I took two steps up and slid one step back. It was slow laborious going. It was so steep that in places I was on all fours, nearly crawling. The pain in my knee was now getting excruciating. I made about 10 or 15 vertical feet up and needed another break to rest my knee. I found a passable place to sit and rested. Pooch had not went ahead as was his habit. He followed me up the slope and when I sat down he went down the hill and sat. First looking at me then looking down the path we had just taken as if to say, "This is far enough Lloyd, let's go back." It was curious behavior for Pooch who never wants to go back. I shrugged it off and continued the climb.

When I rose to continue up, Pooch started back down the route we had just come, went about 30 feet then turned back to look at me. I understood that he wanted to return to the truck. I didn't understand why. Again I shrugged it off and continued on my way up, Pooch following behind. Each time I gained 15 to 20 feet up then rested 5 to 10 minutes and each time Pooch repeated his urging to go back down. It took nearly an hour to gain the ridge-top, but we made it. I took my pack off and Pooch and I shared a snack and water. I took a long break, taking in the view and considering my situation. Pooch sat beside me.

On the northeast of the ridge was a cliff that fell off nearly vertical about 30 to 50 feet to a large crater. The crater was the smaller of two glacial cirques that were on the mountain. The larger one was on the north side, a steep-sided lava ridge separates the two. During the last ice age that began to wane 10,000 years ago these cirques were each filled with a glacier that ate away at the mountains north and northeast side and even lowered the original summit of the mountain. The mountain was once well over 10,000 feet instead of the 9495 feet it is today.

In the distance to the northeast was the sparkling waters of Fourmile Lake and a few smaller lakes and ponds. As my eye followed the ridge up to the summit I could see that except for increasing steepness as you neared the top, the hike would be easier. There were fewer boulders than I had encountered below. From here on the ridge-top was hard pack cinders and sand interspersed with an occasional boulder or lava crag.

I decided to continue my climb and to look for an adequate place to camp if my knee wouldn't allow me to make it to the top. I got my pack on and with the help of my walking stick stood up. Pooch started down the ridge while turning his head to see if I was coming. He still wanted to go back.

Walking was easier now. It wasn't as steep and I wasn't struggling through loose cinders. I made it to about 1000 feet below the summit and saw a passable camping spot near the cliff side of the ridge. It was a small flat spot on the edge of the cliff with just enough room to set up my tent. I took a break to consider my options.

As I sat there I saw two climbers descending from the summit. They must have started after us and passed us while I had been sidetracked. When they got to me we chatted for about ten minutes. I told them my plans to camp on top and how that somehow I had hurt my knee. I ask them about the hike to the summit. They told me it got steeper and would be a real tough hike with a heavy pack and a sore knee. They then continued down the mountain.

I took the pairs advice to heart and decided to set up camp here, then continue to the summit without my pack. I wanted to reach the summit. It would be terrible to get this far then go back without reaching the top. I had hiked with pain in the past and felt confident that I could make it.

I took Pooch's pack off. This would normally be the time he knew he was free to go exploring. Off he would go making about a ¼ mile circle around camp chasing away any bear, deer, coyote or anything else near our camp. But not today. Today he went down the trail a short distance and sat and pouted. He didn't want to stay. He wanted to go home.

I began to set up camp. The only level spot was near the cliff and when I got my tent spread out the north edge of it was within a foot of the edge. I knew that it wasn't unusual for high winds to come up suddenly at this elevation and I didn't want to be sleeping on the edge of cliff in a tent that wanted to sail off. Somehow I had to anchor it solidly to the mountain. The four corner tent pegs are what anchor the tent. Once I got them driven in the loose gravely soil I realized they wouldn't hold in a high wind. They held while I got the tent erected, but they could easily pull out of the loose gravel in a gale. I found four large rocks about 20 or 30 pounds each and placed one on top of each peg to keep them anchored. I hoped they would keep me from flying of the cliff in the middle of the night. After arranging my ground pad and sleeping bag I put all of my gear in the tent, zipped it up and took a long break. Pooch and I shared another snack and water.

I grabbed my walking stick, camera and canteen and started up the mountain. I hadn't gone far when I came to a large snowdrift on the north side of the ridge. I stopped and put snow in my canteen.

I would have ice cold water when I reached the top. Without my pack my knee still hurt but it was better. As we neared the summit it got steeper, but it wasn't near as bad as I imagined from talking to the two hikers. We made the summit in about 30 minutes. I spent about a half hour on top taking in the view and taking pictures. My walking stick has a camera mount on it, and my camera has a timer so I managed to get a picture of me and pooch together in spite of the fact that all he wanted to do was go back down. I felt good. The alpine breeze was magnificent. We had overcome the pain and obstacles and now stood on the summit!

Going back down was in some ways harder than going up. My knee got jolted more and it was easy to twist it with downhill strides. When we made it back to camp I decided to eat supper early. It was a Monday and Monday Night Football would be on at six. I had brought a small portable radio and wanted to listen to the game because my team, the Seattle Seahawks, were playing. I set up my one burner white gas camp stove and got some water boiling. To that I added my homemade dry ingredients for chicken and dumplings. It was one of my favorite back-packing meals. While my dry ingredients were boiling I made a batter for Bisquick dumplings. Then I got out Pooch's dish and filled it with two cups of dog food. I dipped into my chicken soup and poured some of it over his food. It would make a tasty meal for a dog, but Pooch wasn't interested. He had been sitting about thirty feet down the ridge from me and pouting. Food couldn't entice him. He still wanted to go down the mountain.

I put the dumplings in and was soon eating a tasty filling meal. Pooch finally couldn't stand it and returned to eat his meal with me. After cleaning up I got some water boiling and made instant coffee. With my back to a boulder I relaxed as I drank my coffee and smoked a cigarette. I was feeling good. My knee didn't hurt as long as I wasn't walking.

Shortly before six I went in the tent, stripped down to shorts and tee shirt, crawled in my sleeping bag and began searching for the game on the radio. In an unusual move, Pooch came in the tent and curled up at my feet. He rarely slept with me while hiking. The only times he would is when it was pouring down rain or when the mosquitoes were so thick you took them in with every breath. Radio reception at that altitude was awesome and I soon found the game. With my clothes as a pillow I settled back to enjoy.

As the sun was getting low I stepped out of the tent to take a leak. I was taken in by an unusual sight. I saw a dark triangle that spread a hundred miles across eastern Oregon. At first I was dumfounded. What could it be? Then it hit me. It was the shadow of the mountain I was on! I got my camera and began taking picture as it crawled across the high desert of eastern Oregon. I was mesmerized and watched until the sun went down in the west. Reentering the tent I crawled in my bag and immediately went to sleep, missing the remainder of the game.

I awoke at dawn with the radio still on. Setting my stove outside I put on a pot of water to boil, then dug out Pooch's food and fed him. I made a cold cup of Tang and drank it while the water came to a boil, then made hot chocolate and two packets of maple flavored instant oatmeal. I had breakfast in bed!

I dressed in the tent and stepped out in the sparkling cool morning air. The morning view was beautiful, but my knee had stiffened overnight and it was painful moving around. I was anxious to be going so I hurriedly broke camp and repacked. Once more I struggled to get Pooch's pack on while he squirmed with excitement. He sensed we were now going down the mountain.

It was slow going down the ridge. I was careful to not take too long of strides lest I twist my knee and damage it further. Pooch led the way staying very close to me. So close in fact that I often had to poke him with my walking stick to clear the way. I wasted no time sightseeing and taking pictures, we were anxious to get off the mountain. With frequent rests it took about an hour to reach the point on the ridge where we left it and went down to the trail through forest. Once down to the trail Pooch became excited and twirled in circles. As we rested he rolled on his back while I scratched his tummy. He was a happy dog!

As we went down the trail Pooch reverted to his old habit of running far ahead, returning occasionally. On the smooth trail-tread

I was able to make better time and we were back at the pickup in about another hour and a half. Taking the pack off for the last time was a relief and after getting Pooch loaded I got in, started the engine and headed for home. I had brought the beer to celebrate our successful climb but didn't feel like wasting time at that moment. Once down the Four-Mile-Lake road we were on Highway 62 which is a pretty busy road with lots of cops patrolling so I didn't want to crack a beer there. It's only about ten miles to the Butte Falls turn-off on Rt. 37 and I was there in no time. Once on Rt. 37 I opened a celebratory beer and continued the journey home.

As I traveled I reflected on my friend Le Pooch. I am convinced that he knew that I was injured on our trip up the mountain and when the pain became excruciating is exactly the moment he began urging me to end the trip and return to the pickup.

How did he know? Something in my voice, something in my movements, or did I give off an odor that I am not aware of? I don't know, but I do know that he knew and was concerned for my safety. Thousands of years ago dogs were wolves living in packs. The survival of the pack was dependent upon the safety of each individual and each individual was protected by the entire pack. Those instincts were not lost when dogs they were domesticated. Pooch was doing his duty as a faithful pack member. And like most dogs he was incredibly adept at reading the silent signals I transmitted without my even knowing it. I am forever amazed at the ability of dogs and I am forever grateful that Le Pooch cared for my well-being on our many travels together.

Shortly after we returned home I saw a specialist about my knee. I had torn a ligament and with extended rest it might heal. If not, surgery would be required. After about a month and a half of light use it did finally heal. Le Pooch was right. I should have turned back.

I knew a lady who was an artist. Her specialty was portraits of animals. I ask her if she would do one of Le Pooch and she told me she would come to my home and take some photographs of him to use as a guide. We spent a couple of hours sitting in our back yard one day trying to do the impossible; get a dog to pose. After about ten shots she ask me, "Does he always have his tongue out? I've been trying to get a picture of him without his tongue out but haven't been able to yet." A few weeks later she had his portrait finished and we were happy with the results. We paid her about $200 dollars for her work and I spent another $80 getting it framed. Below is a photo of that portrait.

Le Pooch died in 2005. I was heartbroken and you could see a grown man cry whenever I saw something that reminded me of my hiking companion. We thought so much of him that we had him cremated. We took his ashes to the Blue Canyon Trailhead and walked the trail about 200 feet until we were within the  Sky Lakes Wilderness Area then I spread his ashes alongside of the trail. As I left I made a promise, "Someday I will be here with you Pooch, and we will go hiking together again."

Every year since I have went to the trailhead to visit Le Pooch.

The End